BEYOND PROFIT

BEYOND PROFIT

The complete guide
to managing
the nonprofit organization

* *

by FRED SETTERBERG
and KARY SCHULMAN

1817

HARPER & ROW, PUBLISHERS, New York
Cambridge, Philadelphia, San Francisco, London
Mexico City, São Paulo, Singapore, Sydney

Designed by Ruth Bornschlegel

Library of Congress Cataloging in Publication Data

Setterberg, Fred.
  Beyond profit.

  Includes index.
    1. Associations, institutions, etc.—United States—
Management. 2. Voluntarism—United States—Management.
3. Fundraising—United States. 4. Charity organization.
I. Schulman, Kary. II. Title.
HV91.S38 1985   361.7′068   84-48192
ISBN 0-06-015472-1

89 RRD 10 9 8 7 6 5 4 3

This book is dedicated
to our parents and families:

SPENCER AND ELEANOR SETTERBERG

MARK, SUSANNAH, SARANELLA, AND SAUL SCHULMAN
AND HELEN KISTER

CONTENTS

* *

Appendix A
NONPROFIT TECHNICAL ASSISTANCE
ORGANIZATIONS
page 251

Appendix B
COLLEGE DEGREE PROGRAMS
page 254

Bibliographic Notes
page 256

Index
page 263

ACKNOWLEDGMENTS

* *

We owe a great debt to a large number of people working in the nonprofit sector who shared their experiences, insights, problems, and skills. In particular, we'd like to thank the following people for their time, criticism, and advice.

Mark Greenside, Melinda Marble, Rick Smith, Richard W. White, Jr., Jo Menefee, David Landis, Helen Drotning-Miller, Patricia Wilson, Ernest Landauer, William B. Cook, Carolyn Walen, Sherri Roberts, Charlene Harvey, Suzanne Lilienthal, Christine Feidler, Lonny Shavelson, David Robins

The general formula of management for the future might be—think globally and act locally.   —*René Dubos*

BEYOND PROFIT

* *

THE WORLD OF NONPROFIT ORGANIZATIONS

Life in the independent sector

We are born for cooperation, as are the feet, the hands, the eyelids, and the upper and lower jaws.
—Marcus Aurelius

This book is about getting things done. It's based upon the conviction that our cooperative effort can yield startling results. We believe that men and women, inspired by common purpose, equipped with energy, vision, and skill, can combine to change the world. In other words, we are writing a very realistic book.

Throughout its course, we'll hammer away at the notion that nothing is more important than understanding precisely what it is that you hope to accomplish. And pursuing that theme, we'll attempt to locate the commonsense tools of nonprofit management that separate mere good intentions from effective action. Given the crucial role that many nonprofit organizations now play in shaping the life of our nation, it's a distinction that we cannot afford to miss.

For the most part, we'll be talking about the nonprofit sector's relatively small organizations—the hundreds of thousands of groups across the country that operate with annual budgets of $500,000 or less. Here we'll find some of society's most adventurous and productive work just getting started.

And here we'll also locate the expertise and commitment that can inspire our own efforts.

FIRST THINGS FIRST. What Is the Nonprofit, Voluntary Sector?

The nonprofit sector is less a world than a universe—vast, varied, and unexplored. Even the nonprofit sector's exact size remains something of a mystery. For the official record, government statisticians point to the 323,000 groups that have actually received the blessing of tax-exempt status from the IRS. Other observers remind us about the myriad less formally organized groups which touch the heart, soul, and pocketbook of almost every American community—the unincorporated associations, which may number as high as three million.

This is a universe which includes both Harvard University and the day-care center around the block from your home. Its fiscal breadth ranges from the multimillion-dollar budgets of the world's finest hospitals to the barely balanced checkbooks of patient-centered support groups. Today nonprofit organizations own at least 10 percent of the nation's property; they employ 10 percent of the population, and spend more than $80 billion each year. More important, nonprofit organizations tackle the jobs that might otherwise be left undone; they breathe life into dreams deferred. "For not a few," writes Waldemar Nielsen, the perceptive scholar of nonprofit organizations, "they even represent what makes life worth living, death worth facing, and the country worth defending."

What unites this diffuse amalgam of groups and aspirations? Above all else, we find that essential, elusive ideal: the "public good."

Uncommon Aid for the Commonweal

When the French writer Alexis de Tocqueville arrived upon our shores in the mid-nineteenth century, he noticed a striking difference between ordinary Americans and their European counterparts.

"The Americans," he concluded, "make associations to give entertainments, to found seminaries, to build inns, to construct churches, to diffuse books, to send missionaries to the antipodes; they found in this manner hospitals, prisons, and schools. If it be proposed to inculcate some truth, or to foster some feeling by the encouragement of a great example, they form a society. Wherever, at the head of some new undertaking, you see the government in France, or a man of rank in England, in the United States you will be sure to find an association."

Indeed, the most famous American trait—self-reliance—has always been tempered by cooperation. Common sense informs us that the unaided independence of the early pioneers is primarily a fiction. Without the help of neighbors, the isolated settler faced an extremely hostile environment: Enlightened self-interest demanded, and received, a collective response. And the brightest flower of our national mythology—the ideal that one's lot in life improves in direct relationship to hard work, pluck, and individual initiative—has always sunk its roots into the nourishing soil of association.

Today, according to a recent Gallup Poll, nearly 55 percent of American adults engage in some kind of volunteer activity. That's ninety-two million people "working in some way to help others for no monetary pay." In fact, the past two decades alone have drawn together thousands of citizens whose organizational spurs were won in the special interest movements of minorities, women, consumers, peace, and civil rights. And now these activists have joined thousands of other volunteers to work at the local level, lending their experience to the community efforts that improve the quality of our lives. "What isn't profitable enough for business or popular enough for government," explains Daniel Ben-Horin, writer and manager of nonprofit groups, "that's what nonprofits do."

WHEN IT'S GOOD, IT'S VERY GOOD. The Unique Advantages of Voluntary Organizations

In the life of most nonprofit groups, it has been demonstrated repeatedly that almost everything is possible, given several essential factors:

- Tenacity, desire, and confidence
- A clear sense of purpose (and no hidden agendas)
- Common sense, basic information, and good judgment

If you lack the first requirement, then no book in the world will help. Better now to close up shop and cut your losses. Leave behind the halfhearted efforts, and find something about which you can feel passionately committed. Anything else is a criminal waste; and life is short.

But, if like most nonprofit workers you share the hunger to contribute to our society and the thirst to help move along the necessary changes, then you've probably landed in the right place. For not only does the nonprofit sector offer an exciting, vital position from which to operate, but it also enjoys a number of advantages over both business and government.

Flexibility

In the nonprofit world, small is practical. Our efforts fit snugly between the cracks of American life—oftentimes the best place to get things done. In theory, the limited size of most voluntary organizations enables managers and boards to make quick decisions; to tailor their programs to the particular needs of their clients; to adapt to changes in service demand and funding. In practice, this means that voluntary groups enjoy a better than even chance of remaining human.

A Variety of Approaches

Voluntary organizations prove that there's more than one way to skin a social problem. Take, for example, the dilemma of alcoholism. Alcoholics Anonymous confronts the disease as personal struggle, while investing responsibility for change with the alcoholic himself. Other organizations, like the new wave of temperance groups, seek governmental intervention to raise the legal drinking age. And still others strive to ameliorate the social conditions that encourage heavy drinking; they're concerned with unemployment, poverty, and ignorance about alcohol's effects. While each group may soundly disagree with its counterparts' philosophy and methods, they are all gladiators, armed with different weapons, but struggling within the same broad public arena.

A Strategic Position Between Government and Business

The nonprofit world is variously called the Independent Sector, the Third Sector, and even the Endangered Sector. These epithets also serve as a comment about the nonprofit world's neighbors—business and government.

Consider the big picture from the nonprofit point of view. On one side, at its very worst, we find business: rapacious, insensitive, often irrelevant to people's greatest needs. On the other side, also looking bad, sits the government: vast, stubborn, and maddeningly slow. In our ideal, the nonprofit sector stands center stage—picking up all of society's necessary, often dirty, and always difficult jobs. In some encouraging cases, we even find ourselves acting as program brokers, urging government to undertake or fund areas of service already pioneered by nonprofit endeavors, while easing the business world into a position of support. At our best, we ensure that the important work gets done.

Social Progress, Experimentation, and Continuity

Forbidden access to the corruptingly comfortable seat of power, we are forced to urge, cajole, assail, threaten, pressure, and otherwise push society toward creating more humane goals and institutions. Many of us aspire to "build a new society within the shell of the old." And as marginal entities, we can engage in methods which prove discouragingly risky, unprofitable, controversial, or simply too new for either government or business. Brian O'Connell, president of Independent Sector, urges us to remember that "much of the best volunteering in this country has involved the rabble-rousing Patrick Henrys, Jane Addamses, and Dorothea Dixes of other times, whose unpopular efforts reformed child labor practices, prisons, mental hospitals, and the corruption of 'leaders' of their times."

Moreover, nonprofit organizations serve as a binding force—an ideal training ground for democracy. Here we master basic skills, work closely with people of different backgrounds, and experience the raw power evident in a body of committed citizens. Again, Tocqueville is right on target: "The art of association," he observes, "becomes . . . the mother of action, studied and applied by all."

Access to Private Funds and Volunteer Labor

Our nonprofit organizations are positioned to receive funds from practically every philanthropic hand—from the huge grant-giving institutions to everyday people armed with their checkbooks. Unlike donations to the great melting pot of government taxes, the individual donor's gifts to nonprofit organizations can be specifically directed toward what he believes to be society's most pressing needs and most valuable institutions. As nonprofit organizations, we introduce an element of choice. And in a world characterized by needs so vast that they urge both clients and benefactors toward bland anonymity, this kind of choice encourages generosity and action.

BUT WHEN IT'S BAD . . . Typical Problems of Nonprofit Organizations

However, nonprofits are not the Lone Rangers of community service. They do not right all wrongs, tie up every loose end, fill all gaps, assure that everyone will live happily ever after— and then ride off into the sunset on their mighty tax-deductible steeds. Despite all the inherent benefits, you will not be surprised to hear that nonprofits have some inherent problems. Yet if we review our sector's primary stumbling blocks, we'll find that several prove to be nothing other than nonprofit virtues turned inside out.

A Lack of Clarity About Goals and Purpose

Many organizations don't know why they exist. Of course, administrators may trot out stock phrases about "providing essential services to the inner-city community" or some such lofty banality. But hard questions about local needs, program delivery, and community response often expose glaring holes in the group mythology. Like most organizations, voluntary agencies fall into the trap of believing that their continued survival—usually, no mean feat—is reason enough.

The continuing bad news is that our society harbors a number of conflicting, ambivalent attitudes about the value of volunteer work. The pervasive "bootstrap" theory of self-improvement is still deemed the proper course to success. And the value of charity itself has often been held in dubious esteem, with official skepticism reaching back as far as the Puritan's Humane Society of 1809, which declared that "by a just and inflexible law of Providence, misery is ordained to be the companion and punishment of vice."

Inefficient Management

In general, we lack basic management skills. Even worse, many of us have actually shunned the accumulated knowledge and routine business methods that allow the private sector to function efficiently. Today you can still find nonprofit workers who feel that there is something inherently undemocratic about learning to read a financial statement. And nonprofit managers and boards alike sometimes fear that rigorous planning and evaluation might turn their half-million-dollar community organization into IBM.

Oftentimes we mask our management shortcomings for long periods through sacrifice, evasion, or even willful ignorance of our plight. Hence many organizations seem to be in better shape than they really are. And this helps explain why crisis so commonly disrupts the daily life of nonprofit endeavor: Crisis is most often precipitated by not knowing where you stand today and having little idea of where you'll be tomorrow. In other words, it fills the void left by the abdication of leadership and management.

Insufficient and Undependable Financial Support

Today's hard luck scramble for funding propels administrators toward dozens of schemes, each promising the necessary cash to support their programs, while we play catch-up with runaway needs and liabilities. The fiscal life of nonprofit organizations has definitely grown tougher. And while the fundraising techniques of many groups have become quite sophisticated, almost all of us face added competition, increased consumer demand, and shrinking public resources.

In the meanwhile, foundations continue the charade of offering "seed money" for new projects, when long-term support is really the big question. Corporations jump into the funding fray, oftentimes with enthusiasm. But nobody other than the most naive or craven apologist believes that they will compensate for the enormous cuts in government funding. And for those groups fortunate enough to hold on to their government grants, there remains the frustrating, costly compliance with endless forms, petty regulations, and requirements untouched by logic.

Today the most basic capital expenditures are postponed regularly, leaving many groups to operate with antiquated office machines and ineffectual procedures. Oftentimes there's not so much as a data base or a floppy disc in sight. Worst of all, we must constantly rebuild our organizations as our experienced staff members depart in search of adequate salaries and stable careers. The uncertainty of fiscal support has pushed countless organizations far from their appropriate role in our society. Too often our lives are spent reacting to the world, rather than acting to change it.

Public Invisibility

The question of who will pay for the important services provided by the voluntary sector has yet to be the topic of cogent national debate. In fact, the lack of governmental attention to almost any aspect of the voluntary sector is some measure of how far we have yet to travel to bring our needs before the public. Unlike the military, the steel industry, or even small for-profit businesses, we have no congressional committee charged with the welfare of our sector. We have no presidential advisor, no standing advisory committee. Yet the little we have heard from the highest echelons of government seems to indicate that our elected officials hope to see us somehow compensate for the federal withdrawal from public welfare programs.

Even worse, the general public—including those regularly aiding and aided by nonprofits—fails to grasp our sector's enormous potential. The nonprofit sector is like the nose on our face that gives us character, centers our vision, and enables us to breathe; it seems to have disappeared by sheer dint of its familiarity.

SO WHERE DO WE GO FROM HERE?

Our mandate is certain, if somewhat overwhelming. We operate in a sector that oftentimes can't pay its bills, duplicates services, bungles management, and occasionally doesn't even really understand why it exists in the first place. We must put our house in order.

In the meantime, as we continue to flourish and grow, we must also dare to dream of a fully mobilized nonprofit sector that can pursue everything that government and business have failed to achieve. Our organizations must build international understanding and peace, save our land and rivers, work for full employment, guarantee that no one will ever again starve, wipe out crime and the causes of crime, build strong cultural institutions, and assure that society's most vulnerable members live securely and free from fear. It is, to say the least, a big order. And while there is a nation's worth of distance between some of us on how to tackle any one of these problems, we know in our bones that our commitment as individual citizens united by a common cause is our best bet for the future.

Or in the words of the redoubtable Pogo, cartoon-strip character and great soul: "We are confronted with insurmountable opportunities."

1

* *

ANOTHER KIND OF BOARDROOM

Building a board of directors

All authority belongs to the people. —*Thomas Jefferson*

The Board of Directors is a curious beast. For all its collected heads, it often fails to see straight. Its staple nourishment seems to be the boring meeting; its byproduct, the complicated resolution. The undisciplined, undomesticated Board tends to prowl around aimlessly, alternately baring its teeth or settling into a snooze. It has been known to devour its young.

Yet, there's common agreement that the Board of Directors should inspire, sustain, and drive an organization forward. It should resemble a lioness: ferocious in the pursuit of its goals, yet tender and nurturing toward its offspring. And of course, it must set a noble example within the community.

Why, then, do so many Boards act more like rabid squirrels: weak, but terribly dangerous? What is this hybrid creature that governs our organizations?

BOARD RESPONSIBILITIES. Or, I'd Be Glad to Join, but Do I Really Have to Work?

First, the standard definition. . . .

The nonprofit Board of Directors consists of unpaid volunteers who shoulder your organization's legal, fiscal, and ethical responsibilities. They breathe legitimacy into your enterprise, and chart the organization's course. Your Board is the buck's last stop.

As a tradition, the nonprofit Board is as American as cherry pie. "As soon as several of the inhabitants of the United States have taken up an opinion or feeling which they wish to promote in the world," wrote Alexis de Tocqueville in 1835, "they look out for mutual assistance; and as soon as they have found each other out, they combine. From that moment, they are no longer isolated men, but a power seen from afar, whose actions serve for an example, and whose language is listened to."

The nonprofit Board of Directors embodies the spirit of "mutual assistance." They draw upon their collective wisdom to guide an enterprise in service to the community. They're stewards for the public interest.

But what do they actually *do?*

They:

- Exercise legal and fiscal control
- Raise money
- Ensure sound management
- Retain organizational identity

Legal and Fiscal Control

Individuals band together to tackle the problems that they dare not face alone. In its most formal state, this combination of enterprise and discretion is deemed a "corporation." Think of the corporation anthropomorphically: It is a legal *person*. It has its own name, personality, and vocation. It earns and it spends. It was born, and eventually it will die. In the meantime, it must be clothed, fed, housed, and cared for.

The Board of Directors serves as the organization's legal guardian. At a bare minimum, it constructs bylaws, files the required forms with the state and federal government, meets annually, and guarantees that the organization is still on track toward reaching its avowed purpose. As the lifetime parent figure, the Board also oversees the financial entanglements of its ward. In some cases, Board members, both as a body and individually, may even be liable for an indigent stepchild's debts. To prevent such a dread occurrence, Boards predictably urge hard work, self-discipline, and a clear head about figures. All of this is sound practice—though, as we shall see, insufficient.

In concert with the executive director, the Board approves the annual budget, reviews monthly or quarterly financial reports, and keeps apprised of the organization's fiscal state. Few people relish this chore. But if the Board turns its back on the numbers, it is subject to the charge of extreme parental neglect.

Fundraising

Almost all Boards raise money to support their deficit-financed operations. And here, generosity begins at home. *Every* Board member, in accordance with his or her means, should contribute annually to the organization. No, there are no exceptions. Even a symbolic gift of $5 can help achieve the unanimity of purpose that fires effective Board fundraising. Not incidentally, this kind of commitment also inspires that warm glow of confidence that we like to see from funders. "I always ask how many Board members contribute," said one major community foundation officer. "After all, if they don't give, why should anyone else?"

After the members' gifts are counted, your Board can begin its real work: raising money from outside sources.

"We make it absolutely clear from the beginning," stated one Board president, "that all members assist with the financial life of our organization. They can buy their way out with a substantial contribution, make a dozen pitches to their most generous friends, or work on any of our fundraising projects. But full participation, in one way or another, means the difference between relative organizational health and painful fiscal surgery come midway through the program year."

Ensuring Sound Management

As a Board member, the *least effective way* to promote good management is to do it yourself. Board members simply are not equipped with sufficient time—and often not the skill—to assume managerial duties. And that's not their role either. Rather, the Board hires a chief executive officer who in turn manages the organization. The Board undertakes the difficult task of appraising the executive director's performance; and when it is found lacking, the Board fires him and finds another. This is never easy, but it comes with the territory.

Of course, your Board should *help* its administrator. Contacts, tips, and guidance through managerial mazes are among the appropriate ways by which a Board member can lighten the director's considerable load. For example, while a Board member skilled in personnel selection would probably not participate in staff hiring interviews, she might give advice that will smooth the process.

Retaining Organizational Identity

All too often, an organization's sense of itself remains volatile. And in the early years, this ferment can be yeasty and productive. But finally the Board must assume an *activist* role in defining the organization it presumes to govern. Its members—and it's terrifying to consider how seldom this occurs—must understand, articulate, and stand behind your group's unique cluster of purpose, style, aspirations, and vision.

THE AGENCY EXECUTIVE AND THE BOARD

Role confusion among the Board and staff is one of the chief reasons why organizations bog down in conflict and fail to achieve their goals. Unless this confusion is resolved, your Board will soon stumble, revolt, and evaporate, and the executive will eventually depart. In fact, the relationship between the executive director and the Board of Directors forms the crucial nexus between management and governance—the

balance point upon which an organization either steadies itself
or collapses.

A strong Board, fulfilling its duties, selects a strong executive. She, in turn, hires capable staff. The staff reports to
the executive. Never to the Board. Think of this as a clear
chain of command or, if the military metaphor rankles, just
call it common sense. If your staff regularly appeals to the
Board for direction, then the executive will be laboring under
the impossible burden of responsibility minus authority.

The agency executive belongs at every Board meeting,
and more often than not, at committee meetings. The Board
meeting is the primary location in which a working bond is
forged with the executive. Here, after thorough research and
preparation, the executive takes her problems to the well of
collective wisdom. Here she enjoys the opportunity to impress
the Board (and thus keep her job) with accurate, detailed, rea-
soned accounts of probable future difficulties and possible solutions.

The Matter of Policy

The executive constructs programs and strategies with the assistance of the staff. In this sense, she often sets—to use a
much-abused term—*policy*.

For years the notion of *the staff* setting policy was considered rank heresy. Policy was the realm of the Board. In
fact, this is a popular old saw, but somewhat misstated. The
Board can check to make certain that a counseling agency does
not metamorphose overnight into a recycling project or fast
food outlet. It can approve or reject plans and projects. It can
even reorient the organization's very purpose. But once the
agency's broad goals and specific strategies have been gath-
ered together within the framework of a long-range plan, then
the Board can only sit back and make certain that the manager's policies for operation are safe, sane, appropriate, and
productive.

However, when the executive desires to undertake *an important, precedent-setting policy*, whether in the area of pro-

gramming or operations, then the Board should step into the picture. And, of course, the matter of governance—that is, *the rules* by which the agency is assembled and directed—is always the sole province of the Board.

Again, the executive keeps the bills paid, the employees active, the customers happy: She keeps the whole operation breathing. Is there any other way to say it? *She runs the organization.* The Board's role, in relation to the agency's management, calls for judgment, analysis, and restraint. Board members evaluate the speed, route, and coach-comfort of their organization's long journey towards its ultimate purpose; but they leave the driving to the staff.

A degree of tension almost always exists between the executive and the Board. Together they serve as team members, checks upon one another's performance. Yet, they are unequal partners whose authority and power shifts and fills. And however sharp that edge of tension may at times feel, it's undeniably helpful in firming up an otherwise flabby organization. Think of the executive and Board as engaged in a kind of prolonged isometric exercise. They should press and strain with mutual determination and goodwill. Sometimes they'll jerk and pull and lightly swear under their breath. But beneath the sweaty grimace, they're building the bulk, strength, and muscle that will help the organization survive.

SELF-GOVERNANCE. How the Board Works

This is familiar territory. The roster of standard Board offices has followed us ever since grade school when classroom elections first introduced us to the confusion between popularity contests and democratic process. Yet unlike the elections of yesterday (or national politics today), the careful Board measures its prospective officers not in terms of image or affability but strictly according to commitment and skill. This is serious business. The nonprofit Board is limited in size and thus in flexibility and recuperative powers. One or two poor choices in leadership can put it on the critical list.

The President

When Board meetings seem dull and disorganized, when the agenda is missing, when members contrive to pass an hour in loud and needless conflict, you may then lay the blame in the president's lap. The Board's elected head assumes the enormous task of orchestrating and delegating all Board functions. In fact, the president often personally attends to a great deal of the day-to-day drudgery in order to spare the entire Board from its debilitating effects. She leads, presides over, not to say *manages*, the Board in much the same way that the executive director takes responsibility for the smooth sailing of the agency. The Board itself may very well flourish or perish under the hand of its president. In fact, only a well-established committee system can save a Board from the disaster of an ineffectual head.

Again, leadership does not equal "doing it all alone." Rather, the effective president sets into place the many moving parts that keep the Board running. She assigns responsibilities, praises accomplishment and effort; she sets an example and strikes an attitude that makes shirking unthinkable.

The Vice-President

All the platitudes of conventional politics fit the vice-president's uncertain slot. Yet while the vice-president may have little to handle in terms of weekly duties (unless he can be persuaded to take the chair of an important standing committee), he occupies an ideal place in which to broaden his knowledge while deepening his involvement. This office is the most fertile recruiting ground for future presidents. The vice-president should be selected on the assumption that, if all goes well, he will succeed to that position.

The Secretary

This is an important, underrated role. The secretary takes the minutes for all meetings, has them typed up (or, more often, types them himself), and distributes them to members prior to the next meeting. Usually when this task is efficiently handled—like so many other important jobs—nobody notices. But when the minutes are riddled with omissions and inaccuracies, the secretary (rightly) takes the heat. In fact, in the worst-possible-case scenario, an ill-turned phrase can weaken the official record of Board action in a legal dispute.

The quality of most Boards' minutes is dreadful. But eventually, through some sorry experience, everyone learns the same lesson: Collective memory and shoddy notes are undependable, and reliance upon them is needlessly divisive.

The Treasurer

Conventional wisdom dictates that you select a banker, CPA, or financial analyst as your chief numbers person. And this isn't a bad strategy. Oftentimes the professional can locate information hidden in the corners of financial reports and budgets that would elude a layperson. As important, a treasurer tied to a financial institution is an ally who can vouch for the fiscal credibility of your group should you one day line up for a loan.

However, any responsible Board member at ease with the logic of numbers can perform creditably in this role. The treasurer's main goal is to preside over as few fiscal surprises as possible.

In Defense of Committees

We've all heard the old joke about the camel: It's really a horse constructed by a committee. Humorous, perhaps, but untrue. Or rather, if a committee *was* involved, it must have been contentiously assembled and ineptly led; most certainly its members never consulted the long-range plan.

In fact, most of the legwork of governance has to be handled in small groups. Boards use committees because they provide focus and depth, relative speed of action, and a confidential forum for sensitive matters. Committees study issues great and small, offering recommendations for action; and they serve as catalysts, not substitutes, for full Board review.

In order to function properly, committees require a clear, written mandate adopted by the entire Board; a strong chairperson; regular meetings enlivened by an agenda of important issues; easy access to information; and strict limitations on their ability to act without the approval of the full Board. Small wonder that committees have such a poor reputation— they seldom meet these criteria.

Some people offer bad past experiences as proof that committees are ineffectual. "Anything important or controversial that would come up would be referred to committee," said one disgruntled member of a women's health care agency. "It was then either talked to death or ignored until it had become a crisis."

Statements like this actually speak to the *lack* of working committee structure. To be realistic: Attempts to handle all matters through full Board participation are doomed. Nonprofit Boards must subdivide their efforts. The committee structure gives the brighter, more active members a showcase for their talents. And it hands the president an opportunity to isolate and neutralize disruptive or unproductive members by assigning them to relatively unimportant tasks.

Committee structure varies among organizations, but there are four functions that must be regularly handled:
- Finance
- Fundraising
- Planning
- Nominating

The Finance Committee

This group is ultimately responsible for fiscal control and credibility. Its members study financial reports, loan authorizations, and cash flow projections. They grill the director on the annual budget before introducing it to the entire Board. The committee is staffed by the people with the best analytical minds and handiest calculators.

The Fundraising Committee

In reality, the Fundraising Committee's work is usually orchestrated by the staff, though few staff development officers would be so tactless as to say so. However, all serious criticism of your Board's fundraising performance (including strong-arm measures applied to recalcitrant Board members) must emanate from the Fundraising Committee itself. It is their challenge to persuade the rest of the Board that raising money is not only an organizational and moral imperative, but also satisfying, stimulating, and fun. The Fundraising Committee should be seen as *where the action is* for the most ambitious and energetic Board members.

The Planning Committee

This group forms the nucleus from which the long-range plan is born. In conjunction with the executive director, the Planning Committee first makes preparations to plan; actively participates as the long process evolves; and eventually reviews and approves the effort before sending the final product forward for Board review. (See Chapter 4: Long-Range Planning.) There is a particular kind of speculative intelligence which should always be represented on this committee. "We found," confided one experienced Board member, "that some of our members who were considered 'too idealistic' or 'impractical' were just the right people to give our planning efforts some spark. Planning isn't all hard data and raw figures. It also calls for some dreaming."

The Nominating Committee

If there's a doctor in the house, then the Nominating Committee is it. This is the only committee charged solely with the health of the Board. It keeps an ear to the organization's heartbeat and should be the first to notice an irregular rhythm. The

Nominating Committee is primarily concerned with succession. And this is no small matter. Strong Boards seldom clone without effort, while weak ones always do. Given that the faces will change, how do you ensure the long life of a sturdy body?

Skillfully handled, this committee can be a potent public relations tool, a direct pipeline to people in the community who can be tapped for leadership. "We want members to feel that they're obliged to replace themselves with someone at least as skilled and committed as they are," asserted one Nominating Committee chairperson. "We take the matter of succession very seriously. And it works, because nobody wants to be remembered years later by the fool that they found to replace them."

As chief steward of protocol, the Nominating Committee also sets terms of Board service. It's essential to stagger Board recruitment and terms, so that the entire membership isn't depleted on an annual basis. And members should be elected for at least two to three years in order to elicit their full effectiveness. The election of officers, bylaw emendations, and other internal affairs may also fall within the committee's realm. As the Board's resident physician, the committee is a great believer in preventative medicine.

Other Committees

Sometimes efficiency will demand the formation of other committees. You might need a Building and Grounds Committee if you maintain an extensive facility or negotiate a complicated lease. An *ad hoc* Special Events Committee can aid your fundraising efforts with one-shot benefits. And a Search Committee should be formed to find and screen candidates whenever you replace your executive director.

The point is to make certain that committees do not create unnecessary work, retard progress, or contribute to factional disputes. When a committee has fulfilled its mission, disband it. (The standing committees will never complete their missions. They are charged with organizational breathing, eating, and reproduction—each a task which will continue as long as the organization lives.)

One very useful addition to the quartet of standing committees is the artful blend of committee chairs and Board officers known as the Executive Committee. This group meets monthly to set agendas, review potential problems, and frame the parameters for the discussion of current issues. They save the full Board much time (and numbing repetition) by identifying key problems and tasks.

In many cases, the Executive Committee actually *runs* the Board, leaving the complete membership to participate more fully in fundraising. At the very least, it can save the entire Board from meeting monthly. A functioning Executive Committee should be able to handle the routine chores of governance, enabling the full Board to meet on a quarterly basis, certain that its time will be spent on matters of substance, rather than the picayune and the predictable.

Some Matters of Size and Shape

How large should your Board be? There's no hard-and-fast rule.

A recent survey by the United Way of New York found that the majority of that city's nonprofit Boards had somewhere between twenty-one and forty members. For smaller organizations across the country—those of us operating with an annual budget of, say, a quarter-million dollars or less—there seems to be a marked preference for placing the limit at no more than two dozen members. Larger, more established, and usually wealthier organizations lean toward larger Boards. The reason? Their fundraising efforts demand it.

In any case, the standard is effectiveness. A Board must be large enough to draw upon a variety of perspectives and skills. And it must accomplish its tasks with an equitable division of labor. After all, members don't have to devote their entire lives to the organization. Now and then everyone should be able to refuse an assignment without guilt.

Yet a Board must be small enough to move with speed and grace. The natural-born obstructionist loves a fat, clumsy Board. He can filibuster, stall, and deliberate, and generally make life miserable for everyone who wishes to go home at a reasonable hour.

The best advice is probably to start small and build organically. When your fundraising campaign calls for added energy, add it. When a major donor shows an interest, waste no time. But be aware that it is even more difficult to get rid of poor Board members than it is to recruit good ones. A divorce is rarely amicable.

Advisory Boards

Let's be straight about this: The last thing you'll get from your Advisory Board is good advice. If they're like most "honorary" Boards, then they simply won't know enough about your organization. (And if they really do have that much to contribute, then they probably belong on the full, legal Board.) In fact, we usually add people to the Advisory Board because we're after their money and good names.

But this body can serve a strategic purpose. Oftentimes a valued person won't commit to Board membership, but will allow herself to be lured into reach with a spot on the Advisory Board. (Another variation of this ploy is to invite someone to serve on a Board committee, and hope to later rope them onto the full Board.) Some organizations manage to make even better use of their honorary advisors. Women's Voices, a national network of women writers, enlists the aid of a half-dozen of the nation's finest poets and novelists. They not only lend the organization prestige and credibility with their names at the top of the letterhead, but they also contribute directly to the fundraising effort by holding benefit readings.

But there are dangers. Not a few Advisory Board members have grown irate to find that when push comes to shove, they have no real access to the legal Board, or to the organization. They can't vote. They may even be barred from attending meetings. On the other hand, many funders have tales of calling for references on an organization being considered for a grant, only to be told by an Advisory Board member that she can't recall a thing about the organization or why she lent her name to it a decade ago.

HOW TO BUILD YOUR BOARD. Nuts and Bolts

The first question that arises when you begin to recruit new members onto your Board is: Who can we get? At this point, most organizations behave in predictable, if not very practical, ways. They attempt to enrich their Board by convincing all their friends to join. Or they follow the Chinese menu approach—one member from column A, two from column B. . . . But the fact is that every Board doesn't *have* to have a lawyer, a doctor, and a CPA. Instead, you should look for people who can add to your efforts one or two of the following strengths.

Organizational Skill

The Board's first task is to organize itself. If there's no agreement on the basic rules and procedures of governance, then all hope for effective action is lost. Look for members who can help the Board put its own house in order. Businesspeople, labor leaders, and organizers from other groups are all good bets. "We ambled along in a predictably inefficient manner for years," said a Board member of a Midwestern health organization. "Then we landed a progressive and motivated corporate executive who helped us develop some basic organizational skills. For our part, we showed him that running a community clinic isn't the same thing as selling soap."

Program Expertise

This is not another vote for the continuing tyranny of "experts." In fact, your Board has a responsibility to avoid the vested interests of any one profession and look toward the broadest, most imaginative perspective in setting program goals. However, individuals familiar with your organization's service area can ask important questions, cite evidence from the field, and bring up appropriate issues. (Certainly a Board composed entirely of elderly bachelor businessmen would commit some serious—and, no doubt, some humorous—errors of guidance, timing, and proportion should they be left alone to care for a child welfare agency.)

Constituency Representation

One of the most common mistakes in Board recruitment is to look exclusively toward the people directly served by the organization. On the face of it, this seems reasonable enough. Who better understands the issues? But this approach fails to appreciate the full impact of your organizational mission. For example, an agency engaged in reducing juvenile crime embraces a potentially huge constituency. Not only do the clients directly benefit, but there is also a peripheral payoff for their families, teachers, local businesses, and the man and woman on the street. Any of these people might make good Board members.

On the other hand, you don't want to cut off your natural constituency. Many Boards need members whose authority derives from a *personal* involvement with the organizational mission. Otherwise, the Board will have to look to the executive director on practically every matter of program substance. The goal here is balance.

Community Clout

This is tricky, since it can easily be abused. Obviously you don't want to put local heavies on the Board as window dressing and then find that they have personal power needs that swamp the whole organization. However, people well connected with the press, foundations, government, or prestigious local institutions can be very useful, providing they meet the key criteria of membership: a genuine understanding of the organization and willingness to work for it.

Personal Traits

"I didn't really understand my motivation for joining the Board," said a member of a West Coast organization dedicated to nursing-home reform. "Then one day I looked into the mirror and saw my grandmother's face. She was canny, tough, and committed to social issues. Now she's gone, and I'm taking her place." Oftentimes, the accident of personal experience, temperament, or family background will produce an outstanding Board member. These people are often difficult to locate, but you'll quickly recognize them by their instant dedication and enthusiasm. Board members like this are worth three CPAs.

Why People Join Boards

Board membership typically involves evening meetings, weekend committee work, financial contributions, and a busload of organizational headaches. It seems to be all give and no take. And nobody makes a dime off the deal.

What's going on here? Why do people agree to serve on Boards in the first place?

Scratch any nonprofit Board, and you'll probably find the following underlying motives:

- Desire to help a struggling cause
- Agreement with the organization's principles and goals
- Interest in learning skills and acquiring expertise
- A need to get out of the house once a week
- Interest in expanding one's social circle
- Desire to acquire a higher profile in the community—

and maybe even get one's name and picture in the newspaper

A cynic might call the first three reasons commendable and the last three self-serving. A realist—or at least somebody interested in building a strong Board—would recognize that they are all fine reasons for signing up. Patricia Wilson, a nonprofit management specialist, goes even further: "The most fundamental fact of organizations is that people join and work in them primarily to act out their own personal development issues. It's cheaper than therapy. The sooner we smash the myth that people work in organizations only to 'use their talents,' or 'get something accomplished,' the better."

In fact, almost any reason is a good reason, as long as the first principle of stewardship is also present: A Board member must understand the organization's purpose, and be willing to support its efforts with time, skill, and money. Lacking this, no amount of motivation will serve the interests of the Board or the organization, and the personal agendas to which Pat Wilson alludes will soon predominate over the work at hand.

But How Do We Get Them on Our Board?

No mystery here.

You ask them.

The most powerful entreaty is the most direct: "I believe in this organization. I've given (money, time, effort). And now I want you to join me in giving."

People join Boards because they've been asked by someone they respect. They may not even know the person who is making the pitch, but they believe, at a gut level, that she's got her story straight.

Where do the right people come from? The pool of local talent dried up ten years ago, right? And all the committed people are already overcommitted!

Nonsense.

Begin from a position of strength. Who do your current Board members know? They, after all, should be the best authorities on the rigors of Board action. They're best qualified (and presumably, best motivated) to be scouring the streets for replacements and additions.

Extend your reach. Move gradually away from home. You might track the local political scene, searching for hungry young aspirants to public office. (Many a city council member has served her apprenticeship on a highly visible nonprofit Board.) Ask corporate friends for advice. A company president can provide considerable incentive when he asks a middle manager from his firm to serve on a community Board as his personal representative. And for some people, a similar request from sympathetic clergy, civic leaders, or municipal staff would evoke a positive response. An arts publication in California even tried *advertising* for Board membvers, and after publishing a full job description they got several terrific people!

The point is: Some people are born to be Board members, some achieve membership with a little persuasion, but most people have Board membership thrust upon them.

Putting It All Together: the Recruiting Process

Strong Boards are hammered together out of clear expectations and trust. From the beginning, the Nominating Committee and its new recruit should feel that they are interviewing one another. A spirited, serious, yet informal tone should be established early in the relationship. In the best of all worlds, both parties will sense an opportunity for mutual benefit. Neither side should entirely feel that they are doing the other a favor.

You should conclude the initial interview by filling the prospect's arms with reading matter. (A complete Board packet will contain your organization's annual budget, annual report, anecdotal material covering major programs, current Board list, Board minutes for the past year, and the policy manual explaining Board rules and procedures.) Assign a contact person to answer any questions that might emerge from the reading assignment. A prospect who bothers to study the lot and then ask questions is on the way to making a valuable contribution.

Following the interview, the Nominating Committee faces its most difficult task—the hardnosed decision. It is imperative that the inappropriate prospect be eliminated. On these unhappy, if not infrequent occasions, action should be swift and unsentimental. Thank the prospect for her time and interest, and politely let her off the hook. Chances are that she also recognized the irreconcilable differences.

On the other hand, if the prospect seems promising, she

might then be introduced to the entire Board. By attending a general meeting, she'll gain an opportunity to witness the real work of governance. The Board may then respond to her individually. (This marriage may be arranged in feudal fashion by the Nominating Committee, but it's the entire Board that will have to live with the results, probably for several years. They need an opportunity to at least catch a glimpse of the new mate.) This is also the ideal time for the Board members to introduce themselves, accenting their personal reasons for commitment to the organization.

A simple telephone poll will determine the Board's measure of the prospect. Of course, to a large extent, the Board bases its decision upon the recommendation of the Nominating Committee—the people who've reviewed the prospect's credentials, checked references (informally, of course), and have something more substantial than visceral instincts to work from. However, serious objections by Board members to the prospect's candidacy must now be reviewed, perhaps within a reconvened Nominating Committee. The introduction of any divisive quantity into a properly functioning Board should always be avoided. (Just as the introduction of a dynamically disruptive quantity into a complacent Board might be considered.)

A formal letter of invitation or phone call from the president of the Board officially welcomes the new member into the organization. She's introduced to staff and other organizational supporters, possibly on a social occasion. (Some Boards send out press releases, hoping for a slow news day at the local paper.) But the most important step—in fact, the very reason for all this action, anxiety, and deliberation—is to give the new member an opportunity to produce. Select a logical committee assignment, and then hand her an initial task that is both necessary and achieveable.

The Education of the Board

Programs rise and fall. Staff changes. Goals refocus as fuzzy aspirations are seen in the clear light of experience. Many agency executives, blinded by their own constant involvement, fail to appreciate their Boards' limited opportunities to keep abreast of these new developments.

At a bare minimum, the Board should enjoy a detailed annual review of programs—given by staff for several hours on a weekend—which will enable them to grasp the full dimensions of their organization. At its maximum, this meeting could be a full-blown annual organizational evaluation. Staff might also attend Board meetings on a regular basis, updating their particular program specialties. Whenever possible, the Board should be involved in active, experiential learning. It's always better to see a program in action than hear about it; and it's better to participate, even for a few minutes, than merely watch.

Then there are the basic skills of stewardship. These can be more problematic. Not everyone will join the Board knowing how to read a financial statement. Only a few members will have had any experience in planning. And hardly any will understand the tactics, tools, and rationale of nonprofit fundraising. But this, too, can all be handled in-house. The treasurer can lead a brief, practical workshop on financial analysis using your own monthly statements. The people most knowledgeable in planning, fundraising, and other pertinent topics can follow suit. Or, at this point, you might call for that organizational witch doctor, the consultant.

You can hire a consultant trained to do whatever your Board requires: stimulate discussion, bind together factions, inspire fundraising efforts, impart skills, tips, and techniques of governance, and soothe abrasions of the ego with the salve of his great good sense. But remember, a valuable consultant never presumes to solve Board dilemmas. Rather, he passes along tools, insights, stories, and the confidence that the Board can tie up its own frazzled ends.

WHAT A BOARD LOOKS LIKE
WHEN IT'S WORKING

Boards can fail in fifty different ways. How do we know when things are going right? The scene might look something like this. . . .

At 7:30 P.M., the full Board assembles around a wide conference table. Nobody arrives late. Already spread across the table are taboleh salad, roast chicken from the deli, and homemade brownies. There's coffee and tea, and maybe even a carafe of inexpensive white wine. It's almost a social occasion.

The view from the twelfth story is breathtaking. The Board's resident accountant routinely appropriates his company's conference room for meetings.

The president calls the meeting to order. All present, or at least accounted for. The secretary reads the minutes from the last meeting. Since everyone has already received them in the mail along with an agenda and financial statement, there's little need to dissect their contents. The minutes are, as always, precise and accurate.

Next: the financial report. This lasts five minutes. Again, the members have all reviewed its contents earlier in the week. Their questions are informed and specific. Someone reminds the other members of meetings in the old days when the ritual decoding of financial hieroglyphics ate up a full hour and forty-five minutes.

The president calls upon the agency executive for his report. Of course, he's prepared. (He's probably contributed three hours of study for every scheduled hour of the meeting.) He eases out from the silence that has characterized his demeanor thus far, and offers a report sketching the progress of all the programs with which the Board is familiar—which is to say, all of the programs. At the end, he summarizes a new proposal to extend the geographic boundaries of a particularly successful project. But there are problems. Uncertainties about funding, questions about licenses, zoning, and municipal government support. The Board discusses the proposal. A few eyes light up as individual Board members contribute their specialties—finance, law, political expertise. Finally, the Board agrees that the problem should be relegated to committee. The Planning Committee, along with the executive, is charged with developing a final recommendation prior to the next meeting.

Committee reports follow. The standing committees review their activities since the last Board meeting. When the Fundraising Committee announces its proposed goal for the upcoming membership drive, some of the newer Board members object. The goal seems extraordinarily ambitious. What is its basis? The committee chairperson passes out a summary of the Board's fundraising progress over the past three years. While the Board may disagree with the committee's conclusions, no one can say that it's failed to do its homework.

The other committees offer their reports. All speakers are limited to twenty minutes, unless they have made other arrangements with the president. For the greater part of the meeting, the Board digests and discusses the analytical work and recommendations developed in committee.

Of course, the meeting also allows some flexibility for unexpected events. When a trusted Board member takes a few minutes to sound off about what's been bothering him for some time about the organization, he's listened to by the other members. The meeting serves as a pressure valve, defusing negative comments that might otherwise escape into the community. It is not a bull session, gripefest, or encounter group; but legitimate complaints must be aired.

The meeting adjourns on schedule. All members leave with a clear sense of their duties prior to the next meeting. Nobody arrives home too late to catch the eleven o'clock news.

All in all, it's hardly a dramatic event. But it's not meant to be. These very ordinary and important meetings should spare Board members the high drama of histrionic debate and sizzling factionalism. Indeed, Board members have an inalienable right not to be bored. Their right should be exercised in the real cause of excitement: the pursuit of long-range goals.

Here an important paradox is revealed. At meetings where strife is the rule, the sum of the sound and the fury usually signifies nothing, except an organization headed for trouble. But when meetings work well, what you see is only a glimmer of what you'll get. The excellent Board, like the champion athlete, seems to function effortlessly.

ADDITIONAL RESOURCES

The Effective Board by Cyril O. Howe. 1960. The Association Press, 291 Broadway, New York, NY 10007.

Although written nearly three decades ago, Howe's guide to Board organization and management remains a useful tool. Well organized, readable, and thorough.

Glossary of Tools and Concepts for Nonprofit Managers by Barbara H. Schilling. 1981. The Management Center, 150 Post Street, Suite 640, San Francisco, CA 94108.

In less than twenty-five pages, Schilling covers the major problems of governance for the nonprofit Board. This glossary makes an excellent primer for your new Board members.

2

* *

WHO'S IN CHARGE
HERE, ANYWAY?

Staffing the nonprofit organization

> I think most of us are looking for a calling, not a job.
> Most of us have jobs that are too small for our
> spirit. —*Nora Watson,* quoted in *Working* by Studs Terkel

Of all the stubborn contradictions that beleaguer our sector,
this is perhaps the most painful: We fight for economic justice
and social progress around the world, but we often leave a
terrible mess in our own backyard. Nonprofit organizations are
notorious for their poor working conditions. Anybody who has
been around the nonprofit world for even a short time can
relay all the usual stories about insecure employment, miserly
salaries, and cavalier administrative responses to ordinary personnel needs.

It's shocking. Common sense tells us that the people on
the front lines, the men and women who handle the daily
work—the staff—need to be recognized and respected. At
times, they should even be courted and pampered. But staff
abuse is a tradition in many nonprofit organizations. And in
most cases, the trouble can be traced to three major flaws:

• Lack of clarity about staff roles, authority, and accountability

• Lack of systems to massage, lubricate, enforce, and otherwise evaluate and improve these roles
• Lack of genuine leadership

OF TIME, EFFICIENCY, AND COMMON SENSE

Nonprofit organizations are often likened to small families. And in many cases, the metaphor fits. Unfortunately, we're not always talking about happy families. If you ask disgruntled employees what galls them most about their work, they'll probably mention:

• Recognition—usually too little, even in a high-profile job
• Rewards—often insufficient, even when wages are tolerable
• Power—almost always spread too thin or concentrated among a fortunate few

But of course, organizations aren't really families. For one thing, their reasons for existing are quite different. Nonprofit groups coalesce around an organizational mission; their aspirations extend beyond mere survival; and in any nonprofit "family," everyone from the most beloved administrative matriarch to the humblest clerical cousin will eventually be replaced and forgotten.

Which brings us to the division of labor.

How can we best distribute recognition, rewards, and power among the staff to ensure the success of the organizational mission?

Is It Me or We: Top-down vs. Collective Management

Most nonprofit groups rely upon a hierarchical structure. Generally, the ultimate power is invested in the Board, which in turn hires a chief executive officer, who then enfranchises a limited number of staff members to oversee various tasks.

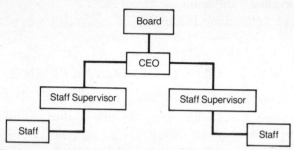

Nobody will claim that this arrangement pioneers new ways of working. Hierarchical management has always been with us. And in the nonprofit world, it's often accompanied by all the usual problems, from organizational dryrot to autocratic self-indulgence. But as a management technique, it can also prove very effective.

"Everybody knows what to do when they come into work on Monday morning," said the director of an advocacy group for the disabled, who employed the pyramid approach. "The monthly objectives are posted, the lines of authority are clear, and by Friday afternoon, we all know who should have planned the previous week for twice the time to get our jobs done."

To be certain, the top-down management style is famous for its advantages. Decisions can be made quickly. The staff is spared the necessity of becoming generalists; instead they may be allowed to hone their skills into needed specialties. And perhaps most important, the location of final accountability, the buck's last stop, is made abundantly clear.

Yet other organizations, particularly social change groups, have experimented with greater democracy in the workplace and report satisfactory results. In most collective structures, emphasis is placed upon mutual accountability, consensus decision-making, and rotating roles.

South End Press, a worker-managed collective and the publisher of more than one hundred books and periodicals, reports that "while our structure has obviously given rise to some errors, it has also been responsible for most of our successes. It has empowered us beyond all expectation, challenged us to be creative and flexible, enabled us to learn an amazing number of skills, and given us the opportunity to produce some important books."

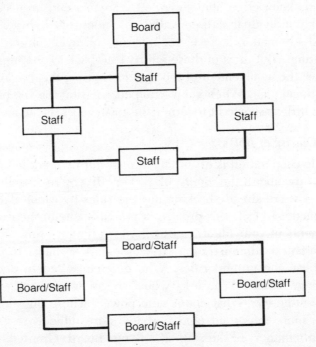

The controversy over hierarchical versus collective management will continue to spark debate within our sector for the rest of the decade. And, most likely, the argument will never really be settled, because, in the final analysis, neither top-down management nor collective organization can deliver the real goods unless several moderating features also fit into the administrative design. The watchword for most small nonprofits is *collaborative management*.

Shared Decision-making

As a manager, every decision you make runs the risk of being wrong, too late, or both. And that's a terrible choice to face each morning: to the right, the need to act decisively; to the left, the necessity of getting the best information and clearest insight. The upshot is this: You're often going to need help, and the best place to start looking for it is with your own staff. Ultimately, you'll be constructing procedures that combine speed, knowledge, and judgment. To this end, you can use weekly individual staff consultations, nonprofit hybrids of the latest "human relations" techniques, or even old-fashioned meetings. But most of these efforts lead back to one important factor: the involvement of the staff in creating the overall organizational plan. When you've helped envision the big picture, it's a little easier to fit together the tiny pieces on a daily basis.

Clarity of Roles

While cooperation is essential, it must not be muddled by uncertainty about the *limits* of power. If you're a collective, fine—you're already hacking out the rules by which decisions are made. In fact, this process is probably one of the essential elements of your identity. But if you rely upon some form of hierarchical administration, then the task remains to clearly establish the ground rules: Who gets consulted in decision-making? When? Who asks whom to get involved? Who has final authority? What about veto power? These questions are even more important (and perhaps more difficult to answer) when members of the staff sit your Board. Granted, this is not an ideal situation, but it happens with some frequency. And in these cases, the division of roles and responsibilities must be crystal clear. Remember, the only thing worse than running your organization single-handedly is to bring staff into your confidence, persuade them that their opinions count, and then go ahead and do what you'd planned to do in the first place.

Communication

Information is also a form of power: Be generous! The fact is that you'll only keep your organization well greased and running smoothly by apprising key people of important issues, conflicts, and opportunities. Regular meetings, crisp memos, and mail routed to all appropriate staff members can ward off the curse of organizational isolation.

Flexibility

When duty calls, the wise executive cleans the coffee pot, scrubs the toilets, and stacks chairs. Or at least, he doesn't habitually pass along the most onerous tasks to everyone else by his divine right of directorship. By the same token, your capable clerical hands may be able to provide useful insights into program planning. (Keep in mind: They've seen it all from a uniquely practical vantage point.)

Staff Unions and Fair Representation

Given that you've constructed the most effective, vital, and democratic organizational structure, you'll still find times when the staff is less than ecstatic about business as usual. For some reason, nonprofit managers and Boards get shook by this reality. In truth, it should come as no surprise that many nonprofit staffs are now organizing or joining unions to further their quest for equitable wages and fair working conditions.

Managers and Boards must recognize their staff's right to organize, and then deal in good faith with their demands. The notion that nonprofit work is a "calling and not 'merely' a job" has been speciously advanced by many nonprofit leaders. Clearly, you don't want relations to polarize into the interests of "management" and "labor." But neither should you extend the worn metaphor of organizational "family" to obscure problems that must eventually be resolved.

To begin, you'll need to dispense with the fiction that the CEO can fully represent the interests of the staff. Keep in mind that the executive's first duty is to the health of the organization. And sometimes, inevitably, the needs of the staff and the needs of the organization will conflict. (Think: How could you simultaneously argue for program budget cuts and an increase in staff salaries?)

In sum, the presence of a strong staff association can help

clarify the needs of nonprofit workers without forcing the executive to play both sides of the street. In some ways, the move toward staff unions and nonprofit workers' rights has only just begun. And with considerable thought and effort, we may be able to strike up the kind of partnership between management and labor that has otherwise eluded both business and government.

Intimate Outsiders: Volunteers and Consultants

If you're lucky, your personnel problems won't end with the staff. Most nonprofit groups eventually attract volunteers—people drawn to the organization because they wish to join the cause. They may arrive on your doorstep due to a plea in your newsletter, a word from a friend, or even a court referral expunging unpaid parking tickets in return for community service. Whether these volunteers prove tremendously useful or a terrible pain in the neck is almost entirely up to you. Before you start counting heads and praising voluntarism, you should ask yourself several questions:

Do We Really Need Volunteers? "Of course," you'll undoubtedly answer. "Every day there are a million chores to complete." But beware: If you haven't actually written down these chores, you're almost guaranteed to forget them when a live body actually crosses your threshold. Organizations require up-to-date rosters of outstanding jobs—the kinds of tasks that volunteers can be directed toward immediately. And these lists should include more than the staple-fold-and-stack jobs. If you really want a volunteer to handle a small amount of weekly bookkeeping, then place that need high on the list. It will encourage you to start looking in the right places.

Can We Spare Anyone to Supervise Their Work? It's amazing how many organizations leave volunteers untrained and untended, as though their work is unimportant or their potential for harm nonexistent. But the supervision of volunteers, particularly during the early training stages, reflects the seriousness with which you regard their efforts. If you truly don't have anyone to handle the supervision, then you probably can't afford to use volunteers. (Or at least, you'll need to search out a volunteer to direct the volunteers.) Untrained recruits, like anyone else whose good intentions have been met with indifference, tend to walk away angry and anxious to spread the news.

Can the Volunteers Handle the Work? Selecting a volunteer is a personnel decision no less serious than hiring a program coordinator. Start off right with a formal interview. (Yes, that takes time. But far less time than hiring and then firing a parade of incapable volunteers.) The interview will only prove successful if you've already considered the skills and personal attributes you'll be needing for the job. Remember that volunteers, if they're going to work with you for more than a few hours, need job descriptions. They're contributing a portion of their lives to your organization, and they're entitled to the same rights and responsibilities as any other staff member. The only difference is they don't get paid.

What's in It for Them? Of course, in the broader sense, volunteers do get paid. They get an opportunity to learn new skills, work among interesting people, develop their self-esteem, and help accomplish an important mission. But like all of us, if their self-interest isn't addressed, they will soon depart. Provide challenges for your volunteers. Encourage their professional and personal growth. Sweeten the most repetitive (and usually thankless) tasks with the effusive praise that they deserve.

Is Volunteer Recruitment a Screen for Larger Organizational Problems? Volunteers handle everything that falls between the cracks—the various, routine, and absolutely necessary tasks that keep an organization up to speed and move forward its primary cause. But they shouldn't pick up the slack of regular staff members who are falling down on the job. Volunteers provide organizational enrichment. They aren't a substitute for paid staff competence. Likewise, volunteers should never, never, never be drawn into labor disputes. Replacing staff with volunteers during a strike is a violation of the trust that must unite paid and unpaid workers. If volunteers are perceived as a threat to the regular staff's jobs, there will be no hope for future cooperation.

Hired Guns: When to Risk a Consultant

A consultant has been defined as an ordinary person who has traveled fifty milies from home. The more generous aspect of this crack acknowledges the consultant's primary strength: She doesn't really know (or have a personal stake in) you or any of your staff. She's free to perform the organizational voodoo that can push a difficult situation back on track.

There are two good reasons for hiring a consultant. The first one is easy to identify. You've got a specific, limited problem—say you're reorganizing your financial management systems—and you need expert advice. The other reason is somewhat knottier. Some organizations call in the learned outsiders when "something" is plaguing their organization, but they can't quite name it. At these times, the capable consultant shakes the organizational tree and then stands back until some recognizable problems fall to the ground.

The rules for selecting a consultant are similar to those for ordinary personnel decisions. Figure out what it is that you want accomplished; then hire the right person for the job. One important difference is that before it's all over you may very well pay dearly for the consultant's advice, whether or not you use it.

So how do you know that her advice will benefit your organization? Or even that she knows what she's talking about?

• Check credentials. Ask about education, training, and experience. (Has she actually *run* an organization; or will you be receiving textbook advice?) And of course, talk to her former clients. In some cases, you'll find that consultancy status is merely a euphemism for "temporarily unemployed."

• Double-check your own purpose for hiring a consultant. Some managers unconsciously set them up as fall guys or outside heavies. Is expert advice really called for, or are you simply engaging a second opinion for a decision you don't care to make alone? If your bookkeeper continues to imbalance your books, you probably don't need a consultant, you need a new bookkeeper.

• Clarify your expectations. What, precisely, do you wish the consultant to accomplish? If your goal is to "reorganize record keeping systems," then think a little harder. How will the new systems improve upon the old? What kind of information will be available? For what end? Strangely enough, many managers expect consultants to magically unravel every organizational tangle and twist, all without knowing what the finished product is supposed to look like.

NOT JUST ANOTHER PIECE OF PAPER. Tools and Procedures for Building an Effective Staff

This section is about everybody's favorite scapegoat: bureaucracy. Or more precisely: procedures. Paper. Writing it down. For the truth is that most nonprofit organizations don't really suffer from extensive bureaucratization, except when they're pushed into it by the government or some other funder. Rather, small nonprofits usually fail to organize their procedures in an intelligible manner. They leave no tracks. And when they get lost, they usually can't find their way back home.

This is a plea for setting your personnel policies down on paper. It will clarify ideas. It will add commitment to good intentions. And best of all, it will provide a point of departure, a place to start thrashing out the various demands of a humane and effective staffing policy.

The Personnel Policy Manual

This is your bible. Everyone should receive a copy. (Some people will actually read it.) The Board can write the personnel policies with help from the CEO and staff. Every couple of years, the manual should be reviewed.

Its pages should grow organically as the need for clarification develops. (If sabbaticals aren't really an issue for your group, don't add pages for the sake of roundness. Let the topic develop naturally, and then deal with it.) But in every case, make sure you've covered the basics.

Employee Definitions

Define full-time and part-time employees in terms of the number of hours they work. This helps clarify who is eligible for employee benefits.

Hiring Practices

Briefly state your hiring procedures relating to advertisement, selection, and internal promotion. Include your affirmative action and equal employment opportunity statements. Check to see if state or federal funding obligates you to formalize other fair hiring practices.

Salaries and Benefits

Include pay schedules, overtime pay policies, terms of merit and cost-of-living raises, and fringe benefit deductions. Indicate state-mandated benefits such as Social Security, disability insurance, and Unemployment as well as the organizational health plan or life insurance.

Working Hours

Specify the minimum hours of work required each week. Include special provisions for flexible time, time off for overtime, sick leave, vacation, and holidays.

Termination

Outline the procedures for layoffs, resignation, retirement, involuntary termination, and final pay. Include grievance procedures, as designated by your Board. The staff must know where it can appeal the occasional injustice or wrongheaded decision meted out by the CEO. And the grievance process also gives the Board a clue when all is not well with executive-staff relations.

Staff Training Plans

Nonprofit workers inevitably pick up a myriad skills, usually mastered on the run, with little time spared for reflection. One of the best ways to add muscle to your organization is to turn this situation around: Devise a formal education plan for each staff member. The point here is to help people grow into new areas of competence and responsibility as they grow into their jobs. Oftentimes, opportunities for professional growth prove more attractive to career nonprofit workers than a marginal increase in the paycheck. Staff training should be important enough to merit its own line item in the annual budget.

Job Descriptions

Good job descriptions are a nuisance to write. They usually require several drafts, a careful review of all tasks regularly performed, and many hours of discussion between the staff and CEO. Then, whenever you undertake a major reorganization, the entire process must be repeated.

But if you don't write, monitor, and revise accurate job descriptions, you soon find yourself working without:

• A fair and agreed-upon standard with which to measure each staff member's performance

• A basis for evaluating the experience and ability of potential new employees

• A precise description of the various tasks which must be completed in order to make your group effective

The best way to handle job descriptions is to ask the staff to write their own. Add to their detailed description of weekly duties the organization's requirements for education and experience. The final document should be agreeable to both staff and the CEO, reflecting the current realities of the job while anticipating changes that may soon affect the position.

The job description needn't be lengthy; any more than

two pages is too much. But it should include: (1) a general description of the position, (2) a detailed list of specific duties and tasks, and (3) a statement about accountability.

An Organizational Chart

The matter of accountability—who reports to whom—is visually clarified in an organizational chart. If your group has grown beyond a half-dozen employees, you should probably review the lines of authority and responsibility on an annual basis, checking for imbalances in supervision and decision-making. A typical organizational chart might look like this.

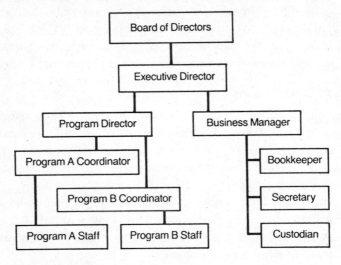

Staff Evaluation Procedures

Evaluation procedures shouldn't be mysterious. When one person sits down to declare your performance adequate or not, there's already sufficient anxiety brewing. The smart manager eases up on this charged situation. After all, you'll want to elicit useful information from the staff, as well as rate efforts and make suggestions for improvement. This can be accomplished only when several questions about the process are answered up-front.

• *How is performance measured?* The job description is

one obvious place to begin. Other criteria should also be explained before you actually sit down and talk.

• *When is performance measured?* Formal evaluations should be scheduled at least semiannually. But keep in mind that the most successful evaluations aren't substitutes for good communication throughout the year.

• *Who evaluates performance?* In most organizations, the CEO will conduct evaluations. Only the Board—and of course, the employee in question—should be allowed to review personnel files once the process has been completed.

The most successful evaluations end up feeling like a dialogue, rather than the final judgment. Information, opinions, aspirations, and disappointments flow across from both sides of the desk. An evaluation that renders staff members passive is almost useless; the point here is mutual engagement. To this end, you can provide staff with a list of the questions that you will be asking them during the formal evaluation. Have them rate themselves. Then use their responses as the basis for your discussion.

Probably no evaluation is complete unless you've touched upon:

• What have been the greatest successes of the past six months? the greatest failures?

• Is supervision adequate?

• Is the job description still accurate and realistic?

• Are relations with the rest of the staff productive and comfortable?

• What will be accomplished between now and the next evaluation?

THE ESSENTIAL INTANGIBLE: LEADERSHIP

These days we hear a great deal about "management styles." That is, not skills, knowledge, or aggregate job performance, but rather, the public display of personality, the mask we assume to get the job done. In fact, a management "style" is oftentimes another word for a personality problem, something best discarded. And it's always a poor substitute for the most crucial element in organizational vitality: leadership. What we must keep in mind is that management and leadership are not the same thing. Management keeps the machine running, and starts from the premise that the values of the organization are immutably cast and undeniably correct. On the other hand, the good leader asks not only how we should achieve our goals, but also *why*.

What, then, are the qualities we look for in nonprofit leaders? They are the same qualities that should characterize our organizations:

- Fair play
- Common sense
- The courage to explore conflicting values and goals

How to Disarm, Dismay, and Otherwise Destroy Your Staff

For a moment, let's look at the leadership problem from the other way around. How would things stand if you were doing everything wrong? What would be the very best prescription for pointless struggle, immense bad feeling, and the rapid erosion of your organization from within?

Should your mind ever take an inexplicably destructive turn, try something like this:

- Encourage the staff to report directly to the Board. This will shatter the natural line of accountability to the CEO and breed resentment and uncertainty in all corners.
- Indulge your mood swings. Inflexibility and unpredictable emotional outbursts are most effectively corrosive when combined in the same person.
- Keep wages low, benefits nil, opportunities for professional growth elusive—and then regularly remind people how lucky they are to work in a nonprofit organization where the problems of the "real world" take a backseat to idealism and informality.
- Speaking of informality, you can let it all hang loose until it veritably droops and dangles to the floor. Let the organiza-

tional files, schedules, evaluation procedures, and merit reviews reflect the clutter of your otherwise-occupied mind. When somebody complains, don't get organized—get angry.

• Make it clear that you're too important to empty the wastebasket, pour someone else's coffee, and otherwise behave like an ordinary human being.

• Never orient new staff members. Let them muddle along as best they can until they make some grievous error. Then publicly criticize their blunders.

• Ignore fair hiring practices as well as your own personnel policies. Illegal and unethical staff recruitment and dismissal is particularly damaging to social action groups.

As you might imagine, the opportunities go on and on. . . .

Some Tracks That Real Leaders Leave

It's difficult to characterize the average nonprofit leader. Behavior, speech, and personal values may vary considerably, even among people within the same agency. But you can best identify the presence of leadership by examining what it has wrought. Within every organization, leaders will inevitably leave their marks.

Teams

Everybody talks about teamwork, but a good leader strives to make it the first principle of staff organization. To build teams that can tackle problems and realize dreams, you'll need to relinquish some control in favor of the collective skills of your staff. That will require a clear sense of group purpose, communication, shared decision-making, and encouragement to experiment and even make mistakes.

Open Debate

Nobody disagrees with an organizational despot, at least not publicly. And as a result, useful analyses get permanently shelved. A smart leader can turn dissent to advantage. After all, a strong objection often indicates passion and a willingness to assume responsibility. Furthermore, a certain amount of controversy (not discord) provides the practical push-and-pull that propels organizations toward their aims. Perfect harmony isn't necessary. Just a willingness to compromise and an agreement to disagree.

Delegation

No true leader does it all alone. Rather, he puts his capable staff to good use by helping to set goals and tasks, and then pointing the appropriate people toward completing them. Consistent delegation of responsibility (and authority) infuses an organization with lasting strength. It gives staff an opportunity to learn from their successes and mistakes, and ensures that an equitable share of the workload (and the subsequent glory) is enjoyed by all.

Plans for Succession

Finally, the responsible leader prepares for her own departure. She's horrified by the notion that the organization won't be able to get along without her. From her first day in office, she's watching for her successor. And more to the point, she's helping the rest of the staff cultivate their own skills and judgment so that the fate of the group does not rest with a single person. Leaders are often said to "emerge" from an organization; you'll find them in unexpected corners. Be ready for them when they first extend a tentative hand. They are the future.

ADDITIONAL RESOURCES

Organizational America by William G. Scott and David K. Hart. 1979. Houghton Mifflin, Boston, MA.

A fascinating study of "the organizational imperative" that powers modern society yet often crushes the very qualities required to lead us from disaster. Particularly strong in its analysis of people working within organizations.

"Administration of Public Interest Groups" by William L. Bryan, Jr. *The NRAG Papers,* Summer 1977, the Northern Rockies Action Group, 9 Placer Street, Helena, MT 59601.

In nineteen pages, the author provides a remarkably thorough guide to the basic problems of staff organization and management. His emphasis falls upon social action movements, though most groups could benefit from the advice.

"Team Building Within Your Organization" by Susan Thomas. *The Grantsmanship Center News,* May/June 1983. The Grantsmanship Center, 1031 South Grand Avenue, Los Angeles, CA 90015.

The mystique of fostering teamwork is reduced to several essential principles readily applied by all administrators.

3

* *

HOW TO AVOID
LOSING $100,000

The artful budget and financial management

Order is Heav'n's first law. —*Alexander Pope*

Nobody can accuse nonprofit workers of lacking ambition. As often as not, our programs take aim at global challenges—all the problems that have plagued civilization for centuries—and promise us steady work for some time to come. Yet, the intricacies of "the big problems" seem to foment less anxiety among nonprofit managers than the less heady concerns of fiscal reports, cash flow analysis, and accrual accounting. Though we may be prove resolute and courageous in the face of countless other perils, many of us turn out to be financial phobics.

TACKLING THE BUDGET

Oftentimes our problems with "the numbers" can be traced back to confusion about the budget itself. What is the budget? It's a document that translates plans into dollars. It ties hopes to realities, serving as a check against our more inflated aspirations. It tells us what we should and should not shoot for; and it calculates our chances of scoring a bull's eye once we take aim. In the life of an organization, budgets break hearts and inspire action.

In short: *A budget is the best possible estimate of an organization's total activity for a fixed period expressed in financial terms.*

By way of a negative appraisal, we can examine what a budget should never be, and yet far too often is.

• A budget is not an immutable law, an ironclad formula. Budgets are written to be changed. They are estimates; and by definition, they fail to achieve absolute accuracy.

• A budget does not reflect the lone vision of the director. Budgets developed in isolation will divide rather than unite organizations. On the contrary, budget preparation provides fertile ground for staff and Board collaboration. And when the Board stamps its seal of approval upon the document, it has formalized a commitment toward the staff taking very specific, quantifiable actions.

• A budget is not a record of what was spent and earned last year, with a little extra tacked on for good measure. The old and infamous technique of adding 15 percent to the previous year's total expenditures eliminates the value of the budgeting process. Instead, the budget should lead managers into the depths of their organization, shedding light through the labyrinth of resource allocation while breaking new trails for agreed-upon goals.

• And finally, a budget is not a report to a funding source. While almost all funders require an annual report on how you've spent their money—and some sources like the federal government or the United Way exact this information in excruciating detail—almost nobody requires the kind of information that contributes to making good daily management decisions. The budget is not a showpiece, but a management tool.

The Budget Preparation Process

The manner in which you construct your budget reveals a great deal about your organization's leadership. The lone executive separated from his staff faces the sorry task of writing the budget without fresh ideas, useful feedback, or alternative takes on abstruse information. On the other hand, organizational collectives confront the frustrating, time-consuming chore of achieving consensus, an effort generally complicated by varying levels of financial acumen. Most organizations, settled somewhere between these extremes, can return to the sharing and debate that marked earlier collaborations in long-range planning.

To begin, the agency director assumes primary responsibility for writing the budget. But he must also engage key staff and Board members to provide data and explain program needs. From the start, he should underscore the relationship of the annual budget to the goals of the long-range plan (see Chapter 4: Long-range Planning). If your long-range plan charts program goals over a period of five years, then the annual budget must reveal the progress over one-fifth of the journey. As the budget process continues, all involved should be deepening their commitment to the long-range goals, or else questioning the original vision that gave them birth.

To facilitate speedy results, the director should convene budget preparation workshops and establish guidelines for staff and Board. ("Since our grant didn't come through, we'll have to postpone purchasing our computer this year, even though it's mandated by the long-range plan.") He'll help the staff determine how much they'll earn and spend during the course of the year. And he'll also lead the discussion that examines the relationship of one program to another and, finally, their cumulative effect upon the entire operation. In the end, you'll find that the budget process appears less like numbers crunching than the artful selection and shaping of hundreds of familiar pieces into a bright, broad mosaic.

The worksheet in Table 1 shows how your staff can evaluate program specialties in terms of financial needs and resources, thus providing the raw data that will help the director construct the final budget draft.

Table 1 PROGRAM BUDGET WORKSHEET

EXPENSES

Personnel

POSITION	MONTHLY SALARY	×	PERCENTAGE OF FULL-TIME	× TOTAL MONTHS = ANNUAL SALARY

1.
2.
3.

TOTAL SALARIES $_____

Fringe Benefits
        Position Title _____
State Unemployment Insurance   __% × __ (total salary) = $____
Worker's Compensation   __% × __ (total salary) = $____
FICA (Social Security)   __% × __ (total salary) = $____
Health Insurance $__/mo. × __ mos.   = $____
Education & Training $__   = $____
                    TOTAL FRINGE BENEFITS $_____
        TOTAL PERSONNEL (including all positions & fringes) = $_____

Nonpersonnel

Rent $____/mo. × ____ mos. = $_____
Maintenance & Utilities $____/mo. × ____ mos. = $_____
Telephone $____/mo. × ____ mos. = $_____
Equipment (list)
_____ $____ (for purchase)
_____ $____/mo. × ____ mos. (for rental) = $_____

Supplies (list)
____/mo. × ____ mos. = $_____
Travel
Local: $____/mo. × ____ mos. = $_____
Out of Town: $____/mo. × ____ mos. = $_____
Postage (Regular & Special Project)
$____ mo. × ____ mos. = $_____ (Regular)
        Special Projects (list)
_____ $____ = $_____

                    (cont'd)

Table 1 (cont'd)

Photocopying
$____ × ____ mos. = $_____

Printing (Regular & Special Projects)
$____ × ____ mos. = $_____ (Regular)
   Special Projects (list)
_____ $____ = $_____

Consultants & Contract Services (specify purpose)
_____ $____

Insurance & Bonding (specify purpose, event, etc.)
_____ $____

Other Expenses (list & specify)
_____ $____ × ____ mos. = $_____

TOTAL NONPERSONNEL $_____

TOTAL EXPENSES $_____

INCOME

Earned

Fees & Admissions (specify activity)
$____ × ____ mos. = $_____

Concessions/Sales
$____ × ____ mos. = $_____

Subscriptions
$____ × ____ mos. = $_____

Rental Income (facilities or equipment)
$____ × ____ mos. = $_____

Memberships
$____ × ____ mos. = $_____

Fundraisers/Benefits (specify)
_____ = $_____

TOTAL EARNED INCOME $_____

Contributed

Foundations (specify)
_____ $_____ (date expected)

Government Grants
_____ $_____ (date expected)

Corporate Contributions
_____ $_____ (date expected)
Other Contributions (specify source)
_____ $_____ (date expected)

TOTAL CONTRIBUTED INCOME $_____

TOTAL INCOME $_____

Summary:
TOTAL EXPENSES   _____
TOTAL INCOME   _____

Analyzing Costs and Income

You've now entered the heart of the budget process. The raw data has been delivered by staff and Board. You're locked in a lonely room with pencil, calculator, and a stack of scratch paper. This is how you begin.

Start computing cost and income estimates. Try to pull together a complete accounting of every dollar running in or out of the organization. And be prepared to fail. Remember, budgets are made up of careful guesswork and flexible estimates. They're tied together with the slender hopes and reasonable fears of organizational imagination. But only by mustering your most precise efforts—that is, by figuring costs generously and income conservatively—can you create the best that can be hoped for: a useful approximation of the fiscal truth.

Costs should be divided into two categories: direct and indirect. Direct costs are expenditures supporting specific program activities. The salary of a counselor employed by a drug abuse center would be a direct cost to the organization's counseling program. Indirect costs include all supporting items that cannot be tied exclusively to a particular program, yet nevertheless make the program possible. Utilities, rent, and bookkeeping would be some of the counseling program's indirect costs. Generally, indirect costs cut across a number of programs or organizational functions, and each area picks up a piece of the service and its corresponding cost.

Both direct and indirect costs seem masters of disguise during the budget preparation process, only to genially unmask themselves deep into the fiscal year. That's why the first step in determining costs should be to consult historical data—namely, last year's books. Review your most recent annual financial statements to locate spending cycles. Post a flag upon continuing liabilities. Note the resources that seem to be drying up. In financial planning, the past is always prologue.

Next, chart your estimates for each budget line item, beginning with personnel. Generally, personnel costs, *the* major allocation in the labor-intensive nonprofit world, are relatively unaffected by the external demands of inflation and market competition. Yet, while the pay standards for nonprofit staff remain stable (read: inadequate), many managers scramble otherwise useful estimates by ignoring internal demands such as:

• Seniority and merit pay raises
• Fringe benefit packages
• Government-mandated hikes in Unemployment Insurance, Social Security, or state disability insurance
• Personnel additions necessitated by program growth

Nonpersonnel items can be traced initially through recent years' purchase orders. These records provide some sense of the range and price of the materials and supplies necessary to run programs. In developing new programs, it may be necessary to solicit bids on program goods and services. Be certain to examine the rate of increase individually for each budget item. Some items, such as office supplies, increase in cost according to the standard rate of inflation. Others, such as rent or equipment, may be secured through a long-term lease or purchase agreement. Others, including utility rates, transportation costs, and contracted labor, move up and down the pay scale under the pressure of market demand and government regulation.

Finally, should you find yourself in the happy position of

having thoroughly delineated all costs for the current year while expecting few program or management changes in the coming year, you may be tempted to simply adjust figures for inflation, compute salary and fringe benefit increases, and combine utility rate hikes with any foreseeable shift in user demand. But let this rule of thumb govern such circumstances: When your first look at the budget reveals few changes from the previous year, take another look, after looking first at your long-range plan. Use the opportunity to refine budget categories and allocations by evaluating each item's benefit in relation to its costs. Admittedly, this can be a rather subjective process, despite attempts to codify cost-benefit analysis. But once again, it will point out the essential question that lies behind every budget: Will a dollar spent here further the goals of our organization—and do we have the dollar to spend?

Types of Budgets

Budgets come in various shapes and sizes, fashioned according to the needs of their makers. However, most nonprofit groups find that their goals and limited accounting resources draw them toward two conventional forms: line item budgets, and program (or functional) budgets.

The Line Item Budget

Most small organizations use a variation of this method (see Table 2). It offers a complete financial blueprint, and even an untrained eye should be able to quickly grasp its message. Using the line item budget, you can determine: how much income can be expected through fundraising; what annual printing charges will total; the sum of administrative expenses versus program costs; and many other useful analyses.

However, the line item budget has limitations. Larger organizations will find that it fails to adequately represent the conflicting needs of their numerous programs or the relationship of various funding sources. The line item budget does not provide the means to compare the income and expenses of

Table 2 LINE ITEM BUDGET

INCOME

Earned Income
1. Counseling Fees		86,870
2. Workshop Fees		3,500
3. Building Rentals		3,000
	Subtotal	93,370

Foundation Grants
4. ABC Foundation		5,500
5. XYZ Foundation		6,800
	Subtotal	12,300

Government Grants
6. Community Development Block Grant		15,000
7. State Office on Developmental Disability		14,000
	Subtotal	29,000

Fundraising
8. Corporations		6,000
9. Individual Contributions		2,000
10. Membership Drive		3,000
11. Special Events		2,500
	Subtotal	13,500
	TOTAL INCOME	148,170

EXPENSES

I. Personnel

Salaries
12. Executive Director		18,500
13. Program Coordinator		16,000
14. Counselors (3)		45,000
15. Secretary		12,500
16. Bookkeeper (½ time)		6,000
	Subtotal	98,000

Fringe Benefits

17.	State Unemployment Insurance	1,020
18.	Workers Compensation	125
19.	FICA (6.7%)	6,566
20.	Health Insurance ($55/mo./7 positions)	4,620
21.	Staff Development	1,000

Subtotal 13,331

SUBTOTAL PERSONNEL 111,331

II. Nonpersonnel

Office & Administration

22.	Supplies	1,400
23.	Equipment Purchase	270
24.	Equipment Rental	400
25.	Postage	2,250
26.	Telephone	2,200
27.	Printing & Photocopy	3,300
28.	Insurance & Bonding	1,550
29.	Dues & Membership	350

Subtotal 11,720

Physical Plant

30.	Rent	10,200
31.	Utilities	3,650
32.	Security	700
33.	Maintenance	2,300

Subtotal 16,850

Travel

34.	Local	250
35.	Out of Town	600

Subtotal 850

Contract Services & Consultants

36.	Auditor	1,500
37.	Publicist	1,200

Subtotal 2,700

(cont'd)

Table 2 (cont'd)

Other Expenses		
38. Contingency Reserve (5% Nonpersonnel Total)		1,600
39. Cash Reserve		1,000
	Subtotal	2,600
	SUBTOTAL NONPERSONNEL	34,720
	TOTAL EXPENSES	146,051
	SURPLUS	2,119

various programs. Thus, one successful program may invisibly carry the weight of several poorly run programs, avoiding scrutiny and mishaping the alignment of the organization.

The Program Budget

Program or functional budgets break down costs and income according to the programs themselves (see Table 3). In this way, you can determine not only the total printing costs for the year, but also the allocations of printing to various organizational functions. You can even distinguish program needs from administrative overhead. Obviously, the potential for comparison and monitoring greatly exceeds that of the line item budget. And as important, the construction of the budget demands a thorough review of each program area, revealing planning gaps that might be passed over through the line item process.

The great disadvantage to the method is the increased bookkeeping time spent following the ebb and flow of separate program funds.

USING THE BUDGET

The artful budget plans for flexibility. During the course of any year, all due to unforeseeable circumstances, funding

Table 3 PROGRAM BUDGET

| | EXPENSES | | | | | |
| | Programs | | | Support | | |
	MUSIC EDUCATION	PERFORMANCES	ART INSTRUCTION	FUND RAISING	ADMINISTRATION	TOTALS
Personnel						
SALARIES						
Executive Director	1,800	2,070	630	2,430	11,070	18,000
Admin. Assistant	2,400	2,760	840	2,700	3,300	12,000
Secretary	1,000	1,150	1,350	350	6,150	10,000
Music Director	8,000	4,000				12,000
Music Instructors (6)	20,000	10,000				30,000
Art Director (¾)			10,000			10,000
Art Instructors			20,000			20,000
Bookkeeper (½)	2,000	500	1,500	1,500	2,000	7,500
Total Salaries	35,200	20,480	34,320	6,980	22,520	119,500
FRINGE BENEFITS						
Mandated Benefits (FICA, Disability, and Unemployment Insurance = 11%)	3,872	2,253	3,775	768	2,477	13,145
Health Insurance ($55/mo./position)	2,871	1,683	2,871	594	1,881	9,900
Total Fringe Benefits	6,743	3,936	6,646	1,362	4,358	23,045
SUBTOTAL PERSONNEL	41,943	24,416	40,966	8,342	26,878	142,545

(cont'd)

Table 3 (cont'd)

| | Programs | | | Support | | |
	MUSIC EDUCATION	PERFORMANCES	ART INSTRUCTION	FUND RAISING	ADMINISTRATION	TOTALS
Nonpersonnel						
Office supplies	800	860	540	460	3,840	6,500
Telephone	600	1,000		600	1,200	3,400
Utilities	700	800	250	300	1,450	3,500
Rent	2,000	1,500	1,500	500	2,000	7,500
Equipment	750	500	250		500	2,000
Postage	100	500	100	700	1,300	2,700
Printing & Photocopy	700	300	1,000	900	1,000	3,900
Insurance & Bonding				500	1,000	1,500
Building Maintenance	300	700	300		1,500	2,800
Audit	300	300	300	300	300	1,500
SUBTOTAL NONPERSONNEL	6,250	6,460	4,240	4,260	14,090	35,300
TOTAL EXPENSES	48,193	30,876	45,206	12,602	40,968	177,845

INCOME

EARNED INCOME						
Instructional Fees	22,000		20,000			42,000
Performance Admissions		17,800	2,000			19,800
Rentals	2,000	3,000			1,000	6,000
Management Fees				2,000	2,000	4,000
Total Earned	24,000	20,800	22,000	2,000	3,000	71,800
GRANTS						
National Endowment for the Arts			7,500		1,300	8,800
State Arts Council	5,000		5,000		4,000	14,000
Community Development Block Grant		2,500			500	3,000
Goode Foundation	8,000				1,000	9,000
Total Grants	13,000	2,500	12,500	-0-	6,800	34,800
FUNDRAISING						
Corporate	6,000	6,000	6,000	2,000	25,000	45,000
Individual	3,000	3,000	3,000	3,000	3,000	15,000
Membership	1,500	1,500	1,500	1,500	1,500	7,500
Events				5,000		5,000
Total Fundraising	10,500	10,500	10,500	11,500	29,500	72,500
TOTAL INCOME	47,500	33,800	45,000	13,500	39,300	179,100

sources may dry up, consumer spending patterns shift, and nonpersonnel costs skyrocket. Your budget must roll with the punches, maintaining the primary boundaries which ensure organizational stability.

The first step is to establish a cash reserve. Some organizations make annual contributions to their reserve by budgeting expenses slightly under what they plan to earn. The obvious objection—"We can't meet expenses now, how can we plan for a reserve?"—will never evaporate until an organization decides that the reserve is a priority, as essential to the organization's health as one of its functioning programs. And indeed, it may very well be that in order to establish the reserve, one of the marginal programs will have to be sacrificed. However, once in place, the cash reserve can serve as insurance against further cuts. The element of fiscal peril, so prevalent in nonprofit life, can be pushed into the corner of acceptable risk.

Beyond planning for flexibility, you must actually *use* the budget as a management tool. Comparison of budget figures with actual income and expenses should be made at least monthly. Significant variances will lead you to ask:

• Whether budget formulations were based originally upon incorrect information

• What, given the new information, needs to be done to readjust the budget? And what will be the effect of budget changes upon the program in question?

• How will budget variances affect the organization as a whole?

• Does the variance indicate that you are not following your long-range plan? Or, in fact, does the plan need changing?

Regular monitoring deters unpleasant surprises. And several tools may assist your analysis.

Start-up Budgets

Most budgets average income and expenses over the course of the year. But in reality, income and expenses prove less accommodating. They do not flow in and out in equal proportions; some months are boom while others are bust. As a result, many organizations find themselves cash-poor during the initial stages of a new program, when expenses generally peak far above income.

A start-up budget, covering anywhere from ninety days to six months, helps alleviate this problem by flagging expenses on a time line. It cites financial and staff resources required to implement the crucial early stages of a program and points out possible conflicts arising from other organizational demands.

Both line item and program budgets can be adapted to the start-up format. Here the challenge is to further refine planning, determining exactly what resources must be utilized and paid for during a limited period of time. A start-up budget should accompany every new program. First, it can serve as a means of determining whether a program is feasible. Then, if you decide to push ahead, it can ensure that the new program debuts smoothly within the context of the entire organization.

Table 4 shows how a child-care agency might plan for the first three months of a new project: an art gallery featuring the work of children from day-care centers throughout the county.

Cash Flow Statements

Cash flow analysis also addresses the problem of irregular receipts, tardy receivables, and unexpected dips in income. As we've noted, although the conventional budget spreads income and expenses evenly over the course of a full year, there may in reality be some months of easy cruising and others marked by desperate straits. Irregular cash flow may prove unavoidable.

However, most organizations can predict their cycles through monthly cash flow statements (see Table 5). These documents enable managers to prepare in advance for cash shortages, taking effective action well before the need for drastic measures intrudes upon daily operations. And under happier skies, they indicate when and for how long surplus cash might be invested in high-interest savings accounts or certificates of deposit.

Table 4 START-UP BUDGET

PROJECT: CHILDREN'S ART GALLERY
PURPOSE: TO DISPLAY THE WORK OF CHILDREN PARTICIPATING IN THE COUNTY DAY-CARE SYSTEM

Budget	30 DAYS	60 DAYS	90 DAYS	TOTAL
EXPENSES				
Gallery Coordinator	$250 (¼ time)	$250 (¼ time)	$600 (½ time)	$1,100
Printing	300 (brochures & publicity)		25 (publicity)	325
Supplies		200 (paint)		200
Contract Services	200 (carpenter)	200 (electrician)		400
Postage	50		35	85
Refreshments/Hospitality			35	35
TOTAL	$800	$650	$795	$2,145
INCOME				
County Art Commission		$500		$ 500
Participating Centers			$150 (10 centers @ $15)	150
TOTAL	—	$500	$150	$ 650
Additional funds required:	$800	$150	$645	$1,495

NOTE: In addition, we will need approximately 65 volunteer hours to accomplish this project.

TASKS:

1. Select gallery site.
2. Print advertising brochure.
3. Secure commitments for artwork from day-care centers.
4. Paint gallery walls w/volunteers.

1. Prepare gallery wall for hanging art.
2. Install lighting fixtures.

1. Advertise show.
2. Prepare opening party.
3. Secure local publicity.
4. Schedule next show.

GOALS:

1. Secure art work.
2. Begin physical preparations.

1. Complete physical preparations.

Open first show.

Table 5 CASH FLOW STATEMENT

		MONTH 1	MONTH 2	MONTH 3	MONTH 4
Cash Out					
Salaries & Fringe Benefits		2,500	2,500	2,500	2,500
Office Supplies		100	-0-	-0-	50
Telephone		-0-	125	-0-	125
Rent		300	300	300	300
Equipment		125	-0-	-0-	-0-
	TOTAL	3,025	2,925	2,800	2,975
Cash In					
Service Fees		2,300	2,300	2,300	2,300
Grants		-0-	-0-	5,000	-0-
Fundraising		550	400	400	300
	TOTAL	2,850	2,700	7,700	2,600
Net Surplus/Deficit for the Month		(175)	(225)	4,900	(375)
Cumulative Surplus/Deficit			(400)	4,500	4,125

FISCAL STACKING AND SHELVING. Your Financial Record Keeping Systems

If the budget guides us toward the promising future, then financial records describe our point of departure. In fact in a well-run operation, the two functions are closely joined. Effective budgets rely upon clear, consistent, adaptable records. Record keeping is predicated upon the demands of financial analysis, usually outlined by the scope of the budget. In sum, the two functions form the nexus from which all financial management decisions should emanate.

But before we examine some basic record keeping tools, let's look at a few of the myths that tend to defeat the efforts of nonprofit organizations at fiscal management.

Myth #1: We Need New, More, and Better Systems of Accounting

It can take years to perfect an accounting system flexible and informative enough to meet the particular demands of your organization. However, the basic method of charting the path of receipts and disbursements can be assembled in relatively little time. Then, if systems repeatedly surrender to internal glitches, you must examine the human element. As with every system, financial records prove only as useful as the reliability of the people involved.

Myth #2: Emphasis on Financial Control Puts Unwarranted Power in the Hands of the Bookkeeper

This proves true only if the agency director abdicates responsibility for financial decisions. That is not to say that the executive should be making entries into cash journals or writing payroll checks, unless, of course, the needs of a very small organization demand it. But the director must have a conceptual familiarity with the bookkeeping system; she should be able to tell when something runs amiss. Furthermore, she should monitor the progress of timely reports to the IRS, state, municipal agencies, and funders. To accomplish this end, the director and bookkeeper should construct a calendar of reporting deadlines based upon the fiscal year, including annual, quarterly, monthly, and weekly tasks. In addition to providing criteria for evaluation, the effort builds organizational memory into the detail-ridden area of fiscal management.

Myth #3: Bookkeeping Is a Waste of Time: It Doesn't Produce Income

Here we hail back to the wisdom of Ben Franklin: Indeed, a penny saved *is* a penny earned. And many of us have learned this lesson the hard way. The history of the CETA program contains thousands of examples of organizations that ended up owing the government money because they failed to justify expenditures on grants received three years prior to the federal audit. One organization told us that during a particularly chaotic epoch of bookkeeping, it chalked up an annual cost of $1,000 in bank charges from checks written against insufficient funds. Or consider the organization that held a $10,000 grant in its checking account for six months, rather than investing it in an insured money market fund drawing a minimum of 8 percent interest. While bookkeeping does not generate income, we must realize that funding sources are not made happy by wasteful mistakes. They are very likely to withdraw support when an organization repeatedly demonstrates its lack of control over financial resources.

Myth #4: Strict Systems of Financial Control Indicate a Lack of Trust

This notion would hardly be worth countering were it not so prevalent among nonprofit workers. In fact, careful monitoring of relatively small amounts of money, such as petty cash, do not reflect Hobbesian gloom about the state of human nature. Rather, controls speak to the vast multiplicity of *good* reasons why hands dip into the pot. (There is always a postage stamp to buy, a parking meter to appease, a cup of coffee to pay back on Thursday.) Beyond the predictability of loss, nonprofit managers must guarantee their public trust. Nonprofit organizations spend *other people's money,* be it foundations, government, or individual contributors. Explicit in the exchange of funds for service to the community is the assurance that all money shall be dutifully tracked and spent only for purposes advancing the cause.

Myth #5: As Soon as Possible, We Need to Add a Financial Person to Our Staff

It seems so obvious, but: Be certain that you have enough work waiting before you hire someone, even part-time, to take over fiscal management chores. It's true that one person in the organization should perform the day-to-day bookeeping. But if the right systems are established and maintained, many smaller organizations will discover that they can keep up to speed with someone already on staff working the books. Remember, there's nothing quite so galling as to watch someone reading the newspaper after polishing off all the tasks that can be assigned.

Myth #6: Computers Will Solve All Our Problems

By the time this book breaks into print, there may very well be an affordable, amiable, desktop machine equipped with appropriate software to meet the entire array of small nonprofit record keeping needs. However, the point remains: Technology should complement organizational needs, not vice versa. Much available software now provides incisive detail regarding unimportant matters, while eluding the essential, peculiar needs of any one organization. No doubt the computerization of payroll can save time for organizations with more than two dozen employees on a weekly pay schedule. But for that matter, so can manually entered payrolls combined to monthly instead of weekly paydays—or even hiring an outside payroll service. The key to evaluating computer services is twofold: (1) Does the computer time (and purchase price) represent a savings over the cost of manual bookkeeping? and (2) Does the automated format provide the specific information that you require to make management decisions? If you can answer yes to both questions, you might try yet another question: Who's going to learn to run the computer?

Myth #7: The Executive Director (or the Board) Must Take Final Responsibility for Financial Management

In fact, no area of management so thoroughly demands cooperation between the executive and Board as fiscal review. The delicate balance between acting overzealously and relinquishing control points up the interdependence of the two roles. Board members are legally and financially responsible for the organization. In theory, they pay the bad debts, possibly out of their own pockets. On the other hand, the executive must be free to manage operations on a daily basis. He can't run to the Board for approval to buy a ream of paper or delay a bill for two weeks. The solution is careful, cooperative monitoring of the fiscal situation, using monthly financial statements written against the format of the approved budget. Monthly cash flow estimates also prove useful in locating the specific needs of individual programs, while further linking cash needs to Board fundraising efforts.

But Why Do We Have To Keep Records, Anyway?

We admit it. Record keeping is a bother and a bore, and nobody in their right mind wants to mess with it. In fact, one of the great advantages of independent nonprofit organizations is their relative immunity to the bureaucratic entanglements of most governmental efforts. To paraphrase Thomas Jefferson: The organization that record-keeps the least, very often record-keeps the best.

Within certain limitations. . . .

To our way of thinking, there are only two reasons to keep records:

• To fulfill legal obligations, such as IRS requirements, United Way reports, or foundation grant summaries

• To analyze your organization's fiscal state in a way that will help you make sound management decisions

The first goal remains rudimentary in design, if sometimes strenuous in execution. The IRS, United Way, state and municipal agencies, and other funders will provide the information you need (and more) regarding their reporting requirements. Government agencies and some other funders, if requested, may even furnish accounting expertise to assist in restructuring your books to ease the strain.

The second goal demands judgment calls. Your records should delineate the journey of every penny received, as it passes into your clerk's hand, winds its way through the accounting office, and finally pops out at the other end as an authorized disbursement. Whether this portrait of income and expense should be drawn in broad strokes or minute detail remains the question that each organization must decide for itself. Remember, time and money demand that you forge from the bookkeeping system only those analytical tools which will regularly enhance your ability to make good decisions.

With all this in mind, let's now look at some basic tools from which you can build your record keeping system.

Checkbook

Small organizations with one or two funding sources and no more than a dozen monthly financial transactions can utilize a detailed checkbook account as their primary set of "books." To maintain an accurate record, all funds received by the organization must pass through the checkbook. This method, amplified by budget categories to track expenses, can show all the critical data of any transaction, charting movement in both income and expense categories. For either area, the important questions are:

- How much?
- When?
- For what purpose?
- From which source?
- To whom?

The single-entry checkbook system offers simplicity and speed for limited accounting needs. Several commercial firms

(Safeguard Systems, Shaw Walker, and others) sell printed one-write checkbook systems that may be adapted to your particular needs.

The checkbook system might look like the one in Table 6.

Cash Receipts/Disbursements Journals

As a substitute for the checkbook method, you might decide to maintain separate journals for cash receipts and disbursements. The journals will clarify financial activity on a daily basis, allowing greater detail and a broader view of your financial activity. And by using the journals, you can easily extract information regarding the entry and exit of money to compose monthly financial statements.

A typical journal page might look like Table 7.

General Ledger

A general ledger combines the information provided in payroll, receipts, and disbursements journals. The ledger enables the manager to quickly summarize financial activity on a monthly basis, paying particular attention to cost control (the amount spent on each item) and budget control (the amount of the budget allocation that has been used to purchase the item). The ledger also simplifies monthly financial statements and clears the trail for the annual audit.

Individual ledger sheets are maintained for each item. Disbursements are handled on separate pages. Information from the journals should be posted in the ledger at the end of each month. (See Table 8.)

Payroll Journal

Payroll information, including taxes and benefits, must be maintained to meet IRS and state requirements. A separate payroll journal proves vital for organizations with numerous employees. Failure to construct and maintain timely payroll records will inevitably result in delinquent payroll taxes, followed by the wrath of the IRS and its penchant for fines.

Table 6 CHECKBOOK

	DISBURSEMENTS/RECEIPTS						FUNDING	BUDGET CATEGORIES					
DATE	PAYMENT TO	DEPOSIT FROM	AMOUNT	CHECK #	BALANCE	PURPOSE	SOURCE	SALARIES	FRINGES	RENT	UTILITIES	PRINTING	OTHER
	CLEVELAND COPY CENTER	ANNUAL BROCHURE	200.00	8	1,000.56 / 800.56		OHIO ARTS COUNCIL					200.00	
		TOTALS											

Your Organization
Address
Telephone

Check #8

Pay to the order of: Cleveland Copy Center $200.00

TWO HUNDRED AND NO/100 ___ Dollars

Jane D. Director
John B. Board, Pres.

Table 7 CASH RECEIPTS/DISBURSEMENTS JOURNAL

CASH RECEIPTS

Journal # _____ Month _____ Year _____ Prepared by _____

DATE	SOURCE	DEPOSIT DATE	DEPOSIT SLIP #	BALANCE	201 WORKSHOP FEES	202 RENTALS	203 CORPORATE	204 MEMBERSHIP	205 GOVERNMENT	206 FOUNDATION	OTHER
			TOTALS								

CASH DISBURSEMENTS

Journal # _____ Month _____ Year _____ Prepared by _____

DATE	PAYMENT TO	CHECK #	BALANCE	101 SALARIES	102 FICA	103 UNEMP.	104 DIS. INS.	105 HEALTH PLAN	106 RENT	107 UTIL.	OTHER
		TOTALS									

Table 8 GENERAL LEDGER

ACCOUNT SHEET

Account: #201 Workshop Fees   Month _____ Year _____

DATE	EXPLANATION	POSTING SOURCE	DEBIT	CREDIT	BALANCE
12/31/84					1,500.00
1/5/85		Cash Rec. J. #10		750.00	2,250.00
1/15/85		Cash Disb. J. #8	200.00		2,050.00
1/31/85		Payroll J. #12	500.00		1,550.00

EXPENDITURES

Account #201 Workshop Fees   Month _____ Year _____

DATE	EXPLANATION	POSTING REFERENCE	TOTAL	SALARIES & WAGES	FRINGE BENEFITS	RENT	UTILITIES	OTHER
	Balance Forward		500.00					
1/15/85		Cash Disb. J. #8	200.00	1,000.00	105.00	450.00	45.00	
1/31/85		Payroll J. #12	500.00	450.00	50.00	200.00		
	Monthly Total		700.00					
	Balance		1,200.00					

Contact the IRS or your bank for assistance if you are uncertain about your liability for taxes, Social Security, Unemployment Insurance, benefits, state disability, and the like.

You Had Better Hold On to What You Got: Internal Controls

Those who merely record the past are doomed to repeat it. Checkbooks, ledgers, and journals all disclose important information regarding financial history. But the challenge remains to *monitor* cash disbursements, and in most cases, reduce them.

All too often, small organizations regard internal financial controls as unnecessary paperwork, or worse, a negative commentary on the staff's honesty and judgment. However, these apparently "small" problems of accountability can gather the collective force to drive an organization deeply, and oftentimes unwittingly, into the red.

Receipt of Cash

Failure to properly account for cash received will quickly erode the confidence of paying clients and vendors. As a simple hedge against disarray and loss, organizations handling daily cash receipts should make daily bank deposits. More than one person must be capable of writing deposit slips, if the bookkeeper does not work full-time. Cash or checks held overnight tempt loss, theft, or more likely, confusion about their origins and purpose. Most banks provide for after-hours deposits for precisely these reasons.

Large or regular receipts of cash also suggest the usefulness of a double-entry receipt system. By passing all cash receipts through the hands of both the bookkeeper and a receiving clerk, you provide a further guard against misuse and miscalculation.

Purchase Orders

Uncontrolled purchases rapidly escalate from small items to numerous small items to the occasional large, expensive white elephant. Necessitated by regularly "unexpected" needs, these random costs reflect planning gaps. A purchase order system will identify these gaps, while limiting expenditures. A simple purchase order system begins with authorized program heads identifying their needs in advance through an item request form. This form can then be checked against budget allocations, approved by the executive or financial officer, and transferred to a numbered purchase order form to be forwarded to the supplier. The numbered form allows for internal reference against suppliers' invoices. No money should be spent without the written authorization of the executive, with budget in hand.

Petty Cash Fund

Expediency inevitably demands quick purchases without the benefit of purchase order controls. The petty cash fund—a small amount of cash designated for such purposes—will enable staff to make necessary purchases on a reimbursement basis. It should be understood that petty cash is merely a *means* of paying for necessary items; it is not a standard expenditure with its own budget line. It follows that all purchases should have the same supporting materials that substantiate purchase orders: receipts, requests for purchases, authorizations. Purchases should be tied to specific budget line items: supplies, postage, etc.

The petty cash fund may be set up with a simple form listing the beginning balance, purchase date, item, amount, and person making the transaction. If working on a reimbursement basis, there should be a column which can be initialed to indicate that the purchaser has been reimbursed. (See Table 9.)

AUDIT PREPARATION

The arrival of the auditor strikes consternation into the heart of the most intrepid bookkeeper. And oftentimes, with good reason. In addition to thoroughly inspecting the accounting

Table 9 PETTY CASH FUND

DATE	PURCHASE ITEM	PURPOSE/PROGRAM	AMOUNT	NAME	REIMBURSEMENT DATE
1/2/84	BALANCE		25.00		
1/4/84	OFFICE SUPPLIES	ADMINISTRATION	2^{75}	ROB. Z	1/10/84
1/6/84	POSTAGE DUE	"	4^{2}	$ SHERRI	1/10/84
1/28/84	REFRESHMENTS	OUTREACH MEETING—	6^{65}	RAPHAEL M.	—
		SUBTOTAL	10.08		
		BALANCE	14.92		

system, the auditor will delve into that large and often shabby area known as "supporting documentation."

Think of your bookkeeping system as a well-constructed argument advancing your credibility as a fiscal entity. Supporting documentation stands behind the system, proof that your argument is based in fact. This means that recepits, timesheets, purchase orders, check authorizations, and other relevant materials must be available. And since auditors charge rates comparable to those of psychiatrists, it makes sense to severely limit their excavation chores by maintaining complete cross-referenced files in all program areas.

At the completion of the audit, ask how the chore might be made easier (and the bill lower) in future years. High audit fees are yet another way in which inadequate bookkeeping doubles back as a financial liability.

FINANCIAL REPORTS. Bringing it all together

In an ideal world, every nonprofit executive would hand his Board monthly financial reports clarifying current fiscal activity and future probabilities. In our less than ideal world, financial reports often fall by the wayside. Or they emerge as complicated tomes, driving a wedge between an organization's "program" and "numbers" people. Misused accounting jargon, variable evaluation methods, and uncertain reporting aims all contribute to the disquieting feeling that basic financial analysis requires an advanced degree in economics and the knowledge of several foreign languages. However, the chief virtues of financial reporting, like most human endeavors, remain simplicity, clarity, and usefulness. The practical financial report will:

• Cover reasonable periods of time, from one month to a quarter
• State all matters plainly, avoiding technical accounting terms
• Reflect budget line items, providing continuity in the overall financial picture

• Provide Board and staff with a common ground for understanding management decisions

Regardless of the form it assumes, the financial report should be able to answer four general questions:

1. What are our total liabilities and assets?

2. What are our specific activities, and how much income/expense do they generate over a given period?

3. How do our actual income and expenses compare with budget estimates, and how much variance can be forecast in the future?

4. What is our current financial position in terms of gain or loss?

The first step in constructing your financial report is to consistently maintain daily journals and the ledger. Your books serve as the sole source of reporting data. Errors in bookkeeping will result in faulty financial analysis.

But the manner in which your books are kept will also affect reports. And books are kept in two different ways: (1) on a cash basis, which records income as it is received and expenses as they are paid, or (2) on an accrual basis, which records income when it is earned or promised (oftentimes many months before it will actually be in hand) and expenses when they are incurred (which may anticipate payment by many weeks or even months). Each system offers its respective benefits. Cash accounting is uncomplicated, and takes far less time. The accrual method provides a more complete and accurate portrait of finances.

Generally, nonprofit groups can blend the two systems to best effect. Expenses should be listed as they occur, giving the full range of organizational obligations. Income should appear in the books only as it is received, taking a conservative view of promises and heartfelt expectations. This modified accrual system hedges the prevalent tendency in nonprofit groups to overestimate income while underestimating expenses.

Financial reports should be readily constructed from your annual budget. Table 10 demonstrates one conventional method of construction based upon the line item budget in

Table 2. It shows figures for the first three months of the organization's fiscal year.

Table 10 FINANCIAL REPORT

INCOME

	July	August	Sept.	Year to Date	Budget
EARNED INCOME					
1. Counseling Fees	6,200	7,100	7,650	20,950	16,870
2. Workshop Fees	-0-	700	-0-	700	3,500
3. Building Rentals	300	400	-0-	500	3,000
Subtotal	6,500	8,200	7,650	22,150	23,370
FOUNDATION GRANTS					
4. ABC Foundation	-0-	-0-	-0-	-0-	5,500
5. XYZ Foundation	-0-	-0-	-0-	-0-	6,800
Subtotal	-0-	-0-	-0-	-0-	12,300
GOVERNMENT GRANTS					
6. Community Development Block Grant	-0-	-0-	5,000	5,000	15,000
7. State Office on Developmental Disability	-0-	2,333	-0-	2,333	14,000
Subtotal	-0-	2,333	5,000	7,333	29,000
FUNDRAISING					
8. Corporations	1,000	2,500	-0-	3,500	6,000
9. Individuals	-0-	-0-	1,000	1,000	2,000
10. Membership Drive	-0-	-0-	-0-	-0-	3,000
11. Special Events	500	-0-	-0-	500	2,500
SUBTOTAL	1,500	2,500	1,000	4,000	13,500
TOTAL INCOME	2,700	5,650	7,450	20,000	148,170

(cont'd)

Table 10 (cont'd)

	EXPENSES				

Personnel

SALARIES

12. Executive Director	1,540	1,540	1,540	4,620	18,500
13. Program Coordinator	1,330	1,330	1,330	3,990	16,000
14. Counselors	3,750	3,750	1,250	8,750	45,000
15. Secretary	1,040	1,040	1,040	3,120	12,500
16. Bookkeeper	500	500	500	1,500	6,000
SUBTOTAL	8,160	8,160	5,660	21,980	98,000

FRINGE BENEFITS

17. State Unemployment Insurance	85	85	75	245	1,020
18. Worker's Compensation	-0-	-0-	32	32	125
19. FICA	547	547	368	1,462	6,566
20. Health Insurance	385	385	275	1,045	4,620
21. Staff Development	-0-	750	-0-	750	1,000
Subtotal	1,017	1,767	750	3,534	13,331
Total Personnel	9,177	9,927	6,410	25,514	111,331

Nonpersonnel

OFFICE & ADMINISTRATION

22. Supplies	350	100	220	670	1,400
23. Equipment Purchase	-0-	400	-0-	400	270
24. Equipment Rental	30	30	30	90	400
25. Postage	130	40	350	520	2,250
26. Telephone	120	110	210	440	2,200
27. Printing & Photo	100	50	1,500	1,650	3,300
28. Insurance & Bonding	-0-	750	-0-	750	1,550
29. Dues & Membership	-0-	-0-	-0-	-0-	350
Subtotal	730	1,480	2,310	4,520	11,720

PHYSICAL PLANT

30. Rent	850	850	850	2,550	10,200
31. Utilities	200	200	300	700	3,650
32. Security	40	40	40	120	700
33. Maintenance	-0-	-0-	-0-	-0-	2,300
Subtotal	1,090	1,090	1,190	3,370	16,850

TRAVEL

34. Local	25	30	20	75	250
35. Out of Town	-0-	-0-	-0-	-0-	600
Subtotal	25	30	20	75	850

CONTRACT SERVICES & CONSULTANTS

36. Auditor	-0-	-0-	2,070	2,070	1,500
37. Publicist	-0-	-0-	-0-	-0-	1,200
Subtotal	-0-	-0-	2,070	2,070	2,700

OTHER EXPENSES

38. Contingency Reserve	133	133	133	399	1,600
39. Cash Reserve	84	84	84	252	1,000
Subtotal	217	217	217	651	2,600
Total Nonpersonnel	2,062	2,817	5,807	10,686	34,720
TOTAL EXPENSES	11,239	12,744	12,217	36,200	146,051
SURPLUS					2,119

The financial report should lead you to ask questions. After reviewing the sample report in Table 10, the wary manager or Board member might wonder:

• Why have foundations failed to produce income during the first quarter?

• How is it that the State Office on Development Disability granted money significantly below the budget estimate?

• What are the implications of spending three-quarters of the Staff Development funds during the first quarter of the year?

• What piece of equipment was important enough to almost double the budgeted purchase allowance?

• Will the lack of maintenance expenditures result in an unattractive or dangerous building or grounds?

• How can audit costs be reduced? Should a new auditor be selected next year?

Of course the answers to these questions will not be found in the financial report. They need to be pondered, and probably researched. The financial report only provides the big picture. Now it's left to the organizational staff and Board to take action. And in a word, that's what financial management is really all about.

ADDITIONAL RESOURCES

Financial Management for Nonprofit Organizations by Leon Haller. 1982. Prentice-Hall, Englewood Cliffs, NJ.

By far the most complete financial guide for nonprofit organizations. Short on accounting jargon and complicated equations, long on practical examples and graphic representations of methods. Recommended for all staff and Board financial people.

Financial Management for the Arts: A Guidebook for Arts Organizations by Charles A. Nelson and Frederick J. Turk. 1975. American Council for the Arts, 570 Seventh Avenue, New York, NY 10018.

Written for arts organizations, this fifty-two page booklet covers the basics of financial management with useful examples that may be adapted to the fiscal lives of nonarts groups.

4

* *

LONG-RANGE PLANNING

The art of implementing vision

Plans are nothing; planning is everything.
—*Dwight D. Eisenhower*

Despite what you may have heard, your organization doesn't need a long-range plan.

That is, you won't be helped by an elegantly bound, expensively printed, carefully assembled assortment of statements, charts, and diagrams that are only going to end up occupying space in your filing cabinet.

In planning, the most common mistake is to focus too much attention upon the final product—the document. But the brightest, thickest, most seamlessly constructed three-to-five year plan is useless unless you've also been able to learn from the planning *process*.

Planning raises problems; it calls upon the planners to offer solutions by constructing a vision of the future, and then pointing out some possible routes to get you there. None of this suggests a static response to the plan itself. Rather, planning is an incitement to action.

Furthermore, there is no *right* way to plan. Any number of methods can lead your organization to a satisfying conclusion—just as they can lead you nowhere. As Richard White, head of agency services for the United Way of the Bay

Area puts it: "It's hard to point to an organization and say, 'They do it right!' The key is not any one structure or style. It's the continuous awareness of the process which causes the entire organization to operate 'planfully.'"

In other words, planning is the complex, never-ending, often contentious task by which you unearth your organization's essential questions, and then encourage the right people to begin answering them.

IF PLANNING IS SO GOOD FOR US, Then How Come We Don't Do It?

A formal long-range plan is the nonprofit sector's new cure-all. No doubt you've heard more than one funder suggest that you better soon produce one of these documents if you're to remain the cherished object of philanthropic interest. Planning is all the rage. No longer will we be allowed to rely entirely upon spontaneity, improvisation, and the undependable flash of enormous insight.

Which is as it should be.

Planning, once adopted as an essential value within your organization, will help you to:

- Focus vision
- Establish priorities
- Recognize opportunities
- Measure progress toward your long-range goals
- Inventory your organizational assets and debits
- Connect aspirations and strategies
- Predict changes within and outside of your organization
- Reduce the necessity for crisis management
- Add a sense of fairness to even the most painful change

You might think that long-range planning would come naturally to your organization. After all, you've been running programs since your inception, and didn't they require plans?

Yes, in fact, they did. But that doesn't mean that you took them seriously. In fact, most nonprofit administrators are extraordinarily *reactive*. They can snap together a passable program within a few hours once they get a whiff of available funding. But they often can't say why the new program is important, or how it will help fulfill the organizational mission. The integrative aspects of planning, which take time, are passed over.

Why does this happen?

Fear of Change and Loss of Power

Nonprofit groups often form around a single strong leader or a strong core group whose personal vision and energy touches all actions. Yet, if the organization is ever to mature and move into a new level of productivity, this "founder syndrome" must be interrupted. Eventually, power and vision will have to be shared. Unfortunately, this often happens in an insensitive way. Initiators of planning may imply that whatever has gone before has less value than what will come after. The PLAN will make everyone more efficient, streamline administration, clean up the organizational purpose, and do everything but windows. Naturally, those who toiled long and hard in the pre-plan years will feel threatened and resentful.

Time and Cost

"We were up to our eyebrows in work on the after-school project when the Board suggested that the most important thing was the five-year plan," complained the program director of a children's agency. "Now I have no objection to planning, but we can't just put everything on hold while we navelgaze. And I think money could be better spent on staff salaries than high-priced consultants with their felt-tipped pens and diagrams fastened to every wall."

Bad Past Experiences

One nonprofit trainer told us: "I've seen these 'plans' abandoned like unwanted kittens. It's criminal when you consider how everybody's hopes were first pinned on their success. The problem is that the plans are often overblown and unrealistic, and then they wind up as examples of how planning fails when they can't be followed." Once a group has this kind of experience, it will usually be reluctant to commit to a second effort.

Public Embarrassment Should the Plan Fail

Just as a plan codifies what you intend to do over a specified period of time, it also reveals what you can't or won't do. Planning can focus a public spotlight upon your organization's direction; and this, in turn, may foment political pressures from the community. "Our five-year plan originally included building a five-hundred-seat performance space which the city really needs," sighed one cultural center director. "However, at this point that seems to be the part of the plan that we're least likely to be able to carry out. The entire arts community is disappointed, because we raised expectations we can't meet. I sometimes wish we'd never showed anyone that plan!"

An understanding must be reached that there will be a place *as a part of the planning process* in which these issues can be raised and resolved. In fact, one of the most important by-products of planning is the opportunity to deal with your group's deep internal conflicts, the essential divisions that have been otherwise obscured by the flurry of daily activity. Planning forces organizational problems to rise so that they can later be skimmed off the top. That's another reason why planning must not be limited to an isolated, single-shot approach, as you might reasonably undertake an annual benefit or the reorganization of your bookkeeping system. Rather, the experience of long-range planning should penetrate every aspect of your organizational design. From programming to fundraising to setting annual operational objectives, you should never be able to say that things didn't go according to plan because there was no plan.

WADING INTO BIG MUDDY. The Planning Process

Before we go any further, we need to say something about the semantic swamp that today mires most planning efforts—that morass of similar terms, which includes "purpose," "mission," "goals," "objectives," "methods," "strategies," and "actions."

The important thing to remember is that these terms refer to *a hierarchy of results*. And while one person may use the word "objectives" in the same manner in which another speaks about "goals," there is less reason to argue about definitions than to understand their ranking in the speaker's hierarchical scale.

For the sake of our discussion, let's rely upon the conventional method of structuring results in the nonprofit world:

1. Purpose
2. Goals
3. Objectives
4. Strategies

The important point is to recognize the relationships among the various levels. At the top, we find purpose. In order to achieve your organization's purpose, you must identify your long-term goals. Goals, in turn, are accomplished after your objectives have been met. And objectives can be reached only by employing various strategies.

Now is that perfectly clear? Probably not. Let's take a more careful look at each level.

1. PURPOSE refers to the ultimate result that your organization is striving to attain. Usually, it's something well beyond the reach of your group alone. For example, the purpose of a community action agency might be "full employment in our community." Nobody really thinks that a single agency will achieve this purpose, but it's crucial to indicate the direction in which the organization is pointed.

2. GOALS reduce the global aims of your organization to a level which you might someday conceivably reach. One goal of the community action agency might be to "increase employment opportunities among minority youth within the community." You'll note that the goal is more specific than the purpose, yet it still lacks a dimension that is precise and quantifiable.

3. OBJECTIVES state your immediate aims in specific,

quantifiable, and time-related terms. The agency's objective for the current year might be to "develop fifty full-time jobs for minority youth within the next twelve months."

4. STRATEGIES refer to your methods, the tasks you'll undertake to get the job done. One method for attaining the agency's objective might be to "negotiate with each local industry for six entry-level slots for youths completing the agency's job training program."

Again, these terms are only useful if they help clarify your thinking. They probably won't line up in a way that feels neat and clean. Your goals and objectives may seem to overlap, and it may be that your statement of purpose needs to be broadened or narrowed once you start piecing together strategic plans. By the end of the planning process, this hierarchy of results should assist you in clearly delineating the relationship between *why* you exist, *what* you hope to achieve, *where* and *when* you'll do it, and *how* you'll get it done.

Before You Get Started: Selecting the Planning Committee

The exact composition of the Planning Committee is anything but hard and fast. It should be determined by using a formula based on energy and leverage. Some people *need* to be involved because of their perspective, expertise, or position within the group. There are others who *should* be involved because they demonstrate enthusiasm and commitment to the process. In any case, while planning to plan, you should consider the following people for membership on the committee:

Executive director: This is a must. There can be no meaningful planning unless the organization's manager is deeply involved. After all, he'll be the person providing much of the data and analysis; and finally, he'll supervise the implementation of the plan.

Board members: Another necessity. Planning only runs skin deep unless the Board is forced to grapple with the essential problems raised by the process. The point of planning is to connect vision with action. For this reason, the guardians of organizational vision, the Board, must be drawn into the process.

Staff: Access to much information (and varying interpretations of past actions) is available from the staff. Moreover, throughout the years, they'll be the people living with the plan—or leaving because of it. They, too, must be included.

Outsiders: Some organizations like to introduce a disinterested third party, someone who cares a great deal about the group and its purpose but grinds no organizational axes. The outsider lends perspective, urgency, passion, and expertise. She speaks for the community as a whole, rather than any one constituency. And within the group, she demonstrates not the slightest desire for personal power.

Facilitator: Another outsider, perhaps a hired consultant, can offer a great deal of help simply by keeping the committee on task. This is a special skill, and you shouldn't expect that just anyone will be able to provide it. Most likely, the executive director, staff, and Board members will not want to sacrifice their advocate's position on the committee in order to assume the neutrality that must characterize the facilitator's role. A few dollars here can be well spent.

How large should the committee be? That's another question open to debate. Less than five probably won't have the time to get the job done, while more than a dozen leads to complications of attendance and coordination, and the increased probability of red herrings.

Planning As Though It All Made Sense

Planning can be messy. In fact, if your planning process does turn out to be crisp, neat, and trauma-free, then you've probably done it wrong. Planning involves change. And while we'll all agree that change is exciting, we have to admit that it's also frightening and sometimes painful.

That said, it should follow that the process itself will probably defy your usual requirements for order and predictability. Generally, planning is approached through a sequential step-by-step routine—which then (if all goes well) tends to unravel somewhere during the middle of the process. For a moment, chaos takes over. This aspect of anxious confusion is important; it can be a crucible for creativity. But it's also necessary that your facilitator prevent each session from running amok. While there isn't one correct way to organize the planning committee, there are several tasks that it must accomplish— often simultaneously.

Task #1: Define Your Purpose

As we have said, most organizations have no idea why they exist. Or rather, they have numerous ideas, many of which conflict decisively. Confusion about purpose runs rampant in the nonprofit sector. Frozen within our reactive postures, it's hard to gather the energy to pull head and shoulders upward, stand on our own two feet, and determine precisely what it is that we hope to accomplish.

Perhaps you think you're different? After all, you've been around for ten years, and everyone knows very well what you're up to. Test yourself. Ask your Board and staff to define your organizational purpose in a single sentence. You'll be surprised at the variety of their responses.

Say you're a service agency for children modeled after the YMCA. Your Board and staff will probably come up with purposes ranging from "providing day-care programs for local kids" to "reducing child neglect, abuse, and delinquency" to "increasing recreational opportunities within the community." And while these notions may all be compatible, their variety in specificity points to a lack of understanding about first principles. What is the one, overall result that you truly want to accomplish? When the hard decisions are called for, what's expendable and what's essential? Where is the organization's soul?

Before you proceed any further, you'll need to answer these questions. (Actually, they're all the same question, posed in somewhat different ways.) One way of coming up with some genuine answers is to sit down and formally write a statement of purpose.

It won't turn out right the first time. In fact, the entire enterprise will probably precipitate waves of confusion, anxiety, and outrage. And unless you've recently dealt head-on with this matter, you'll produce one or two people who not only don't understand, but also thoroughly object to your newly stated purpose. (That's okay, too. This process can be a good way to ease off the obstructionists who've been making your life miserable for years.) But it's only after you've reached consensus about this most basic issue that you can begin the real work of grappling with the future.

Task #2: Excavate Data

In order to decide where your organization should be heading, you'll first have to figure out where it's been. And that means identifying the forces both within and without that shape, squeeze, and otherwise affect your organization.

The first part of your data-mining should be easy. Open up the filing cabinet and withdraw your:

- Annual reports for the last five years
- Financial statements for the last five years
- Historical data on membership, programs, and fundraising
- Mission statements

If you can't produce this information or if it exists only in sketchy form, then you have even further proof that planning is needed. Some organizations go through life with as many versions of these documents as they have funders. That kind of maneuvering only obscures the future.

Next, you'll need to take a hard look at your community. Trips to the library, city hall, census bureau, and the Chamber of Commerce will yield:

- A demographic profile of your service area, including information on your constituency
- An economic summary of the community, including trends among your clients
- A survey of local organizations with goals similar to your own

• An outline of the political and economic forces affecting other community service groups

Try not to get hung up entirely on "objective" data. To construct an accurate portrait of your organization and its community there are also more subjective sources that should put muscle and flesh on your statistical skeleton. These sources might include newspaper and magazine articles, position papers from allied service organizations, or even analytical work by researchers at your local university.

The point here is to collect all the pertinent information that will describe your organization and its crucial relationship to its environment. (If, for example, your group is dedicated to providing English language instruction to Southeast Asian refugees, then you'll want some indication that over the next few years the stream of immigrants will continue to flow into your community.) Be prepared for surprises, and don't merely seek out materials that corroborate prevailing attitudes and perspectives.

Task #3: Argue, Analyze, Synthesize, and Then Summarize

At this point, the planning process gets interesting—and a little crazy. Once everyone has become acquainted with the raw data surrounding your group and community, you'll need to reconstruct this material into a useful form. You'll draw together your strengths, weaknesses, accomplishments, failings, internal aspirations, and external threats.

• What do we do best? Worst?
• Do our programs further our long-range goals?
• Do our goals and programs truly address the needs of our community?
• What are the needs of our community?
• What do community people think about our organization?
• Where is our community heading in terms of population and economic development?
• Who are our clients? What is their economic position?

• To what degree are other organizations competing or assisting with our efforts? Who else is working with our constituency on other issues?

• Who are our allies? Our adversaries?

These questions may once again propel you out into the real world. In this sense, planning is very much a give-and-take process. We extract data from the available resources. We form propositions about the data's significance. We test the propositions through discussion and debate both within the Planning Committee and among interested members of the community. And then we draw our conclusions. Sometimes these conclusions will be disquieting.

Perhaps you'll find that the new education service started with high hopes two years ago is now an organizational albatross. After surveying the community, you may discover that your organization is best known for a program you discontinued five years ago. You might learn that the problem you're so committed to solving is being attacked more vigorously by another group across town.

There's one other important piece of information that should emerge from your game of questions and answers. You should be able to figure out exactly where you'll stand three years from now *if nothing changes.* Allowing for no major shifts in purpose or programming—and keeping your current strengths and weaknesses intact—you should try to summarize the shape of your organization in terms of:

• Programs
• Numbers served
• Costs
• Earned income
• Fundraising programs and goals
• Staffing and Board participation
• Space and equipment

Is this a portrait of your agency moving directly toward its long-range purpose? Your answer will probably be a qualified no. Over the years, even the best-run organization requires fine tuning. (In fact, the best-run organizations thrive upon their regular readjustments; they're realistic about their goals *and* their environment.) And so your (probable) negative answer will lead you to that essential question: *What do we have to do over the next three years in order to get closer to achieving our long-range purpose?*

Task #4: Write Your Plan for the Future

At this point decisions must be made. Call a meeting (or a series of meetings, or even a weekend retreat) to review the assembled information and formulate your goals, objectives, and strategies. You should start off positively. Note your past accomplishments and acknowledge the people who've helped you attain them. But don't bury the fact that you'll want to make changes. At this stage you're shaking hands with the future.

There is no "magic bullet" to speed along this process. For every organizational goal, you'll establish a set of reasonable objectives. For each objective, you'll lay out some specific strategies. You'll construct a realistic time-line. And you'll examine the various opportunities and risks inherent in any new or altered enterprise. In short, following a lot of uninhibited brainstorming and uninterrupted discussion, you'll draw back and take an organizational snapshot of the future that touches upon every aspect of your operations, including:

- Programs and services
- Staffing
- Governance
- Fundraising
- Community relations

The problems revealed by finally committing the plan to paper can be very frustrating. But they can also provide immense stimulation. Planning is the art of dreaming with your eyes wide open. And with the help of your facilitator, you'll now refine those dreams into a precise, quantifiable, time-related organizational scheme. In final form, your plan should be:

- Focused and realistic

- Critical to your mission
- Appropriate to your organizational scale
- Measurable
- Achievable

The plan doesn't have to rival the size of a telephone directory. Nor does it necessarily require elaborate diagrams, charts, and appendices. As always, the simpler the construction, the clearer the writing, the shorter the document, the better the plan.

Task #5: Plug In the Numbers

Finally, you'll need to figure out what the plan is going to cost you. Budget projections provide a reality check on planning. For that reason, they should occur toward the end of the process, when the hard bottom line of fiscal conservatism won't puncture your early, inflated dreams.

Good ideas usually cost money. The task here is to determine approximately how much, when, for how long, and whether your new actions will ever spur new sources of income.

Most likely, your budget projections will send you hurtling back toward the earlier planning stages. Once again you'll have to decide what's essential and what you can't afford right now. Planning is as valuable when it reveals what you can't do as it is when you learn what should be attempted. A firm hand on the calculator will prevent the plan from degenerating into a mere wish list.

With the numbers in place, your plan will inevitably change. Some of the issues that you thought had been buried will come back to haunt you. When this happens, you know that you're planning honestly.

OK, WE'VE WRITTEN OUR PLAN. Now What Do We Do with It?

You've shaped it, shared it, and rewritten the parts that collide with fiscal reality. As far as you're concerned, it's done. But what good is it?

If, like many plans, it's quickly dropped into the nearest filing cabinet, then it's no good, and much of your effort has been sorely wasted. On the other hand, you could be just getting started.

To begin, well-constructed plans can have a gratifying impact upon funders. Foundations and major donors in particular will be pleased to see you thinking ahead, especially if they're primed about the process from the very beginning. Long-range planning shows initiative. And as we all know, initiative attracts its own set of rewards.

Your plan can also be used as a public relations tool. Copies might be delivered to your allies or the people and organizations you're currently courting. An ambitious, honest plan announces you as the up-and-comer that everyone will be watching.

But most important, the plan should assist with organizational evaluation. Remember, it's not the *plan* that's being reviewed, it's your progress towards fulfilling your long-range purpose and reaching your goals. The plan will help focus discussion with greater specificity and detail than you'd otherwise be able to muster. It will light your path into the ultimately unforeseeable future.

ADDITIONAL RESOURCES

Frankly, there's not much written material that's very useful for nonprofit planners. To be sure, you can uncover voluminous appraisals of planning in the corporate world. (Among the best would be Peter Drucker's numerous analyses of management and the occasional monograph, such as George Steiner's "Strategic Managerial Planning," published by The Planning Executives Institute, 5500 College Corner Pike, Oxford, Ohio 45056.) However, among resources specifically aimed at nonprofit planning, the pickings are slim. Everybody talks about planning, but nobody seems to be able to write very well about doing it.

The best hint for most novice planners is to learn from the experience of your peers. Find a local nonprofit group that's successfully constructed a long-range plan, ask for a copy, and then talk with staff and Board members who can tell you what they did right and what they'd do differently the second time around. That said, you might also take a look at:

"Long-Range Process Planning: The First Cut" by William and Suzanne Weber. *The Grantsmanship Center News*, July/ Aug. 1982. The Grantsmanship Center, 1031 South Grand Avenue, Los Angeles, CA 90015.

This article provides an interesting summary of one planning method. It's particularly good on the need to thoroughly survey the outside forces affecting nonprofit groups.

5

* *

FUNDRAISING AS A WAY OF LIFE

Why and how to ask for money

> Is not a Patron, my Lord, one who looks with unconcern
> on a man struggling for life in the water, and when he
> has reached ground, encumbers him with help?
> —*Samuel Johnson*

These days it's very chic—and thoroughly sensible—to talk about increasing earned income levels. We'd all like our organizations to become sturdier financially, more self-sufficient, and less dependent upon the whims and requirements of various funding sources. But then, we'd all like to be rich, too. There's no way to break it gently: For most of us, it just isn't going to happen. In the world of nonprofit organizations, fundraising remains a basic fact of life.

Unfortunately, many of the people who otherwise find enormous satisfaction in their work fixate upon this truth as though it were the *only* fact of life. They lose sight of their group's mission; their vision narrows to the dire consequences should their fundraising goals *not* be met. Naturally, this kind of attitude leads to stress, burn-out, and other hysterical symptoms such as waking at 3 A.M. to make lists.

The flip side of compulsive concern is neurotic inattention, the ostrich syndrome: If you don't notice the deficit, maybe it will go away. But we know better. At the end of the fiscal year, there it will be, elegantly bracketed at the bottom of your financial statement.

Finally, the only sane approach is to embrace the annual shortfall like a valued but difficult relative. Welcome it warmly into the bosom of your organizational family. Understand that it's probably considering a lengthy visit, and start planning how you will care for its varied needs and voracious appetite.

The payoffs can be surprising. Tim Sweeney and Michael Seltzer, two experienced organizers writing in *Community Jobs,* put it well: "Fundraising promotes membership, raises public profile, provides opportunities to build social and political community and enhances organizational credibility. As a result, to view one's fundraising efforts as merely revenue generators is shortsighted."

WHY PEOPLE WANT TO GIVE TO YOUR ORGANIZATION

Over the past twenty-five years, our country has witnessed the growth of a large industry built around our individual and collective reluctance to ask a stranger for a buck. Professional fundraisers and "development" specialists now offer seminars, strategies, and sage prescriptions for locating donors and extracting the full measure of their generosity. The task of fundraising has blossomed into a science.

But let's face it: Most of us still feel funny asking for money. We don't like to think of ourselves as beggars. Our pride, propriety, and plain good manners trip us up. In short, we misperceive the time-honored traditions that legitimate and support our fundraising efforts.

In fact, the motivations for organized giving are deeply rooted within our culture. The Bible, Talmud, Koran, Book of the Dead, and Buddhist scripture all suggest, in the words of the 4,000-year-old Babylonian Code of Hammurabi, that "justice be done to widows, orphans, and the poor." At least one modern observer has added to these moral prescriptions a scientific bias for cooperation that is tinged with poetry. "I maintain," writes Dr. Lewis Thomas, ". . . that we are born and grow up with a fondness for each other and that we have genes for that. We can be talked out of that fondness, for the genetic message is like a distant music and some of us are hard of hearing. Societies are noisy affairs, drowning out the sound of ourselves and our connection. Hard of hearing, we go to war. Stone deaf, we make thermonuclear missiles. Nonetheless, the music is there, waiting for more listeners."

The question for nonprofit organizations is how many listeners will be willing to pay the piper? Or more precisely: What can you do to make them write a check *today* for *your* organization?

Actually, beyond the ethical inducements, there are dozens of reasons why people give. But for our purposes, only one reason counts. Consider the standard rationales:

• We give because it makes us feel good; it enhances our self-image as generous people.

• We give to appease the fates for our own good fortune, to ward off bad luck, to assuage guilt.

• We give to receive something tangible: a gift, a favor, a tax write-off.

• We give to support the causes and institutions that make a difference in our lives and the lives of those we care about.

• And finally, most of all, we give because the right person asks in the right way for the right thing at the right time.

This is the essential lesson of fundraising: *In order to receive a donation, you must ask for it*. Funds are *not*, in fact, raised. They are solicited, requested, demanded, cajoled, enticed, and inveigled.

IN SEARCH OF THE DIVERSIFIED FUNDING BASE

As recently as ten years ago, fundraising was a very different game. Most organizations rose and fell according to a predictable cycle of need. Good ideas were usually fed by volunteer labor. Attractive program efforts were supplemented with foundation seed money. Success was finally ensured by the receipt of a healthy-sized government grant. Finally, when the money ran out, as it always does, watchful administrators leapt onto another three-year funding spiral. Or, as often as not, they closed up shop.

In many ways, the process was even less reliable than today's frustrating scramble. In the past, organizations often grasped for available grants by contorting their goals; or they simply minted shiny new ones. New groups materialized overnight to compete for Washington's latest funding boon. Very few people, particularly among the leaders of small organizations, seemed to think much about continuity in fiscal planning.

In the 1970s, life began to change. As government support rapidly eroded, most administrators soon realized that their reliance upon a single funding source placed their entire operation in jeopardy. We soon harkened back to the folk-wise admonishment of basic production: Anyone who puts all of his eggs in a single basket is guaranteed to trip in the barnyard. Suddenly, our sector discovered the diversified funding base.

These days government and foundation funding continues to fall dramatically short of covering the standard nonprofit deficit. And it's unlikely that we'll see any revolution in funding in the near future. To flourish, nonprofit groups must now look to a variety of fundraising methods that may have previously seemed too complicated or mundane: direct mail campaigns, raffles, memberships, canvassing, personal recruitment of individual donors, and a trail of similar devices.

In return we'll be able to count on:

• Sources of money to turn to in emergencies
• Independence from the priorities of any single funding source
• A positive image of the organization spread broadly throughout the community
• The peace of mind that comes with having options

THE ANNUAL FUNDRAISING PLAN

Fundraising grows from the heart of an organization. It requires imagination, consistency, and probably more teamwork than you have ever mustered in the past. It also requires *a plan*. Here nonprofit managers often err on the side of spontaneity. They fail to recognize the relationship of one fundraising project to another. They treat each income-producing venture as an enterprise with no prior history and few implications for the future.

In fact, fundraising is an essential part of your operations. It's not merely the means by which you accomplish your primary goals, but also a reflection of the spirit and precision with which all other tasks should be completed. Fundraising often presents your most public face. And any competent effort will make demands upon all your organizational resources. You'll soon understand that to raise $10 you may have to spend $2. (Don't forget to budget for the membership drive's printing costs, the new phone lines, overtime hours for the development director. . . .) In addition to these wholly practical concerns, there are several other reasons why you should rely upon a formal plan.

• Too many organizations muddle along with vague aspirations to raise a hefty lump sum real soon. As an antidote to flabby generalities, the fundraising plan sets taut, quantifiable goals. It budgets time, dollars, and staff for specific activities. In other words, it sets a standard by which you can decide whether you've succeeded or failed.

• Personal relationships dominate fundraising. People give to people, not just to causes or organizations. But while good fundraisers must be encouraged, trained, and nurtured, only the fundraising plan provides a *structure* which you can then revise, refine, and replicate. The plan may even prove some small consolation when the development director with the Midas touch (and all the contacts) finally leaves.

• The best fundraising builds upon itself over the years. Small donors become large donors. Avid supporters rope in their friends. This kind of growth isn't accidental; it's subtly, quietly orchestrated.

How to Write Your Fundraising Plan

Fortunately, the annual fundraising plan is a good deal easier to complete than most of the other planning documents that will eventually cross your desk. Like other exercises in logical thought and organizational delivery, it's written for and by the people primarily involved with its execution. It should be positive, accurate, and free from jargon.

Finally, if the plan is to be useful, it must represent the victory of process over paper. You're not aiming to construct a lengthy treatise to be filed away and forgotten. Rather, the plan is a tool for daily use; it will help direct and then monitor your progress toward specific ends. Fundraising is everybody's job. The plan should serve as the glue holding together the various styles and devices employed by your Board and staff.

The plan's first draft is usually tackled by the agency executive in collaboration with the staff development director or the chair of the Board's Finance or Development Committee. At the end of the process, many hands will have touched the document. And as you no doubt recall, that's what planning is all about.

Step #1: Back Up and Construct Your Case Statement

Before you do anything, make certain you know *why* you need to fundraise. That is, why other people should want to give money and time to your organization and why you and your Board must do your best to accommodate them. Your fundraising case statement can be distilled from the long-range organizational plan. In the abbreviated version used for fundraising, your case statement should include:

• A brief summary of the organizational mission
• A sketch of the proposed and continuing programs that need financial support
• Annual program objectives and demographic or statistical evidence to support your service claims

- An estimate of program costs
- Future plans for your organization

Try to limit the case statement to two or three pages. For the most part, this portion of the plan will be reserved for internal use. It'll keep you on track and help explain to new staff and Board members what it is, precisely, that they are working so hard to achieve.

Step #2: Delve into Past History

Now you'll need a broad overview of your fiscal requirements and funding potential. Consult the financial reports for the past three to five years to identify trends. Is foundation funding rising or falling? What grants and contracts are about to come to an end? How stable over the long run is each source? What would be the result of losing any one funding source? (Remember to consider ancillary services, like administration and rent; they're often included in grant awards.) Exactly how much does each fundraising project cost in terms of labor, time, and supplies?

Try to use the information culled from the recent past to patch together conclusions about the probable future. Your annual financial reports provide the most useful clues to whether you'll be able to fill your current fundraising needs. They should ease you toward realistic goals and sway you from betting on miracles.

Next assemble the backup data that you'll use when contacting individual donors and other funding sources. Most of these documents should have already been compiled in the course of your daily operation. If not, take the time now to organize copies of your:

- State and federal tax exemption forms
- Current Board list with institutional and business affiliations
- Current year operating budget
- Financial statement or audit for the most recently completed fiscal year
- Comparative budget summaries for the past three years

• Letters of endorsement
• Most current annual report
• List of grants, donors, members, and other fundraising accomplishments
• Organizational brochure, publicity reprints, or other information that reflects favorably upon your efforts

Step #3: Analyze the Steps in Each Fundraising Project

A healthy fundraising program employs many different tools. Over the years, even a small organization can develop a whole battery of effective devices, including:
• Grant proposals written by staff
• An annual membership drive
• Appeals to corporate donors
• A special event or benefit
• Pitches to local service clubs
• Raffles, yard sales, or other "grass roots" techniques
• Solicitations of major donors

Of course, this kind of variety takes time to build. It also takes practice and craft to make each pitch effective. The best way to plan for a multifaceted fundraising campaign is to adopt a *marketing* approach. Concentrate upon the reasons why each group of donors may *want* to help you out. Given a wide range of potential funding sources, from the Lion's Club to the Office of Health and Human Services, these reasons will prove numerous, varied, and perhaps conflicting. It's your job to appear to be many things to many people without sacrificing your organizational integrity, which *is* a neat trick. But you can probably pull it off if your organizational mission is sturdy and your fundraising tactics are precise. (See Chapter 8, Survival Tactics, for more detail on marketing.)

To begin, you'll need to pinpoint the various tasks involved in completing each fundraising project. For example, you won't be able to simply launch a membership drive one day without preparation. Long before your appeal letters hit the post office, you'll have to cull the names of potential members from your records, write a sparkling solicitation letter, print your pledge card, and complete a half-dozen other jobs.

All of these tasks need to be trailed on a time-line. People within your organization must be given specific duties. Try to identify the positions responsible for each job, but avoid actually naming staff and Board members. Ultimately, that's a management decision that may blow several ways before the plan is set in place. Give yourself optimum room to rearrange assignments, while still committing the organization to an ambitious strategy.

In the end, your analysis of the various fundraising tools should provide a detailed guide so that even a stranger (or a new Board member) can enter the scene and understand your plan.

Step #4: Set Your Fundraising Goals

Now, at last, we get down to the numbers. Once you've selected your fundraising tools, delineated their various strategies, constructed a time-line, and assigned tasks, it's time to specify just how much money you hope to raise. That's where the historical data once again proves handy.

Remember, your fundraising plan should inspire, not overwhelm the Board. You can strive for modest, obtainable goals by calculating your fundraising's average rate of increase over the past three years. Then hold yourself back from committing to anything above a 5–10 percent raise unless you have an extraordinary commitment in hand. Dreaming, in this case, only proves self-defeating.

Step #5: Get Started

The plan is merely paper until your Board and staff are committed to carrying it out. Once you've constructed a good working draft, submit it to the appropriate Board committee. Share it with staff. Work over the fine details and achieve consensus in committee *before* it's submitted for full Board approval. Naturally, the details of the plan, as with all fundraising information, remain strictly confidential. All those involved at this point must be trusted for their discretion.

The best person to introduce the plan to the Board is a powerful and respected member, perhaps the president or the Finance Committee chair. The point here is to make certain that Board members have an opportunity to contribute to the plan, which they will ultimately implement. They must also be kept from rejecting a useful document or getting unproductively stuck on inessential points.

If you have recruited a number of new Board members, or if you haven't taken this integrated approach to fundraising before, you might consider hiring a top-notch consultant to kick off your campaign. Often one or two sessions with an outside professional can get the organization charged up in a way that in-house people cannot. And finally, that's exactly what your campaign requires. Planning brings you to the fabled fork in the road. Now you must draw upon all the enthusiasm, commitment, and good instincts of your organization to help you select the golden path.

ADDITIONAL RESOURCES

"Survival Planning for the '80s: Fundraising Strategies for Grassroots Organizations" by Tim Sweeney and Michael Seltzer. (Originally published in *Community Jobs*, now available as a single document from Community Jobs, 1520 Sixteenth Street N.W., Washington, D.C. 20036.)

Two canny organizers provide a broad philosophical and strategic overview of fundraising for community groups, which can be adapted to almost everyone's needs.

The Grantsmanship Center News, 1031 South Grand Avenue, Los Angeles, CA 90015.

This monthly magazine on nonprofit funding and management is the best available resource for organizations of all sizes. If you're going to subscribe to only one trade publication, make it the *News*.

Foundation News, 1828 L Street, N.W., Washington, D.C. 20036.

If you're going to subscribe to two publications, you might also consider *Foundation News*, which examines the philanthropic scene from the funder's perspective.

6

* *

FROM EXXON TO YOUR
NEXT-DOOR NEIGHBOR

Where the money is and how to get it

Lack of money is the root of all evil.
—*George Bernard Shaw*

The smart fundraiser doesn't waste time. She knows you can't get blood from a turnip, water from a stone, or money from an empty pocket. Instead, like the best investigative reporters, she completes her research, cultivates her sources, follows the trail of the money, and then asks the right people in the right way at the right time. It's that easy—and that difficult.

Examination of the conventional sources—foundations, and federal, state, and local government—reveals that most funding levels are static or declining. But there are other possibilities. A potentially huge source for nonprofit support is sitting in the armored vaults of our nation's major businesses. And to a larger, if less concentrated extent, it's squirreled away in the bank accounts of you, me, and the guy next door. These are the two great untapped, misrepresented, and misunderstood funders of the 1980s: corporations and individual donors.

THE AGONY AND ECSTASY OF THE PRIVATE SECTOR

Deep in the heart of the nonprofit fundraiser, there are two factors motivating the quest for corporate support: overwhelming need and an elementary sense of justice.

In recent years, nonprofit Boards have been teased and titillated with the promise of corporate funding. It's easy to understand why. The potential resources for giving are gargantuan. Since corporations can write off up to 10 percent of their net income, it stands to reason that they can, if they choose, alter the shape of American philanthropy. Of course, promises have abounded, some flying straight out of the Oval Office itself. And in one sense businesses actually *are* increasing their support for the nonprofit sector. While corporate donations have for forty years hovered around 1 percent of total earnings before taxes, the actual dollar amount of donations has more than tripled over the past twenty years.

But put yourself in the average Board member's place. Imagine that your nonprofit organization operates alongside a relatively small chemical plant. Last year you almost broke even, while the chemical plant accrued profits in excess of $5 million. You provide valuable services to community members, many of whom are the chemical plant's employees and their families. Over the years, you have earned a solid reputation for responsible service, while the chemical plant is regularly taken to task over pollution, health hazards, and poor employee relations. Naturally you start thinking: Why shouldn't the chemical plant give us some of that 5 percent net income that the federal government allows them to write off annually? (They can afford it.) Why shouldn't they buy some good will in the community by supporting a service of proven value? (They certainly need it.) And why shouldn't we be willing to accept it?

In fact, these are the questions that must be answered before you go knocking at the corporate doors. To keep our own priorities straight, let's deal with the last question first.

Can You Afford to Accept Corporate Donations?

Some years ago there were a number of extremely productive and important organizations that would no more accept money from business than shake hands with the devil. The words "sell out" were frequently heard as groups debated whether to risk tainting their independence by accepting industry's filthy lucre.

At the time, many of these feelings were quite legitimate and appropriate. But now, for good or ill, we have entered a period of much less suspicion regarding the private sector, and much more accommodation to its demands. This has partly come about as a matter of survival. But it has also been the product of a more flexible and realistic sense of the possible within the nonprofit community.

The fact is that most productive organizations now have enough faith in the integrity of their work that the specter (or appearance) of corruption holds few terrors. In addition, business has not proven the willing buyer of hearts and minds it was once expected to be.

Of course, sometimes the match between a particular business and nonprofit group will not be a good one. An organization working on the environmental hazards of offshore drilling is unlikely to have much success soliciting contributions from Mobil Oil. (And it would find even greater difficulty explaining the contribution to its constituency.) A better partnership might draw together local merchants whose tourist business is affected by oil spills polluting the beaches. Getting money from businesses and corporations does not mean that you have to remain uncontroversial. Rather, it demands that you market your particular controversy to sympathetic funders.

In the end, only you can determine if business fundraising is appropriate for your organization. And here your own attitudes must be frankly appraised.

• Are there people in your group who generally consider businessmen to be exploiters enriching their stockholders at the expense of workers and the public?

• Do the people in charge of fundraising consider your organization *entitled* to corporate money? (The "all we want is our fair share" approach will have catastrophic results.)

• Does your organization frequently use businesses as negative examples in your public statements?

If so, beware private sector fundraising.

There probably are some projects which, for their own integrity, should *not* raise money from businesses and corporations.

This section is not for those organizations.

However, do not think that because your organization seeks social change, or because you serve a specialized constituency, or because you're a poor people's coalition, or minority, or grass roots agency, that you are automatically barred from business funding. In truth, your identity can often shake out all the reasons why businesses *should* support you. And that's what we'll talk about in a minute.

The Business of Business Is Business

For many years, the idea of corporate philanthropy sounded like a contradiction in terms, exemplified, at its worst, by the image of John D. Rockefeller passing out 30,000 dimes in the streets of Manhattan. In fact, in 1881, the high court declared that "Charity has no business to sit at Boards of Directors qua [in the function of] charity." This prohibition set the discomfiting tone that characterized private and independent sector relations until 1935, when federal legislation finally approved corporate contributions. "Modern conditions," explained the court, "require that corporations acknowledge and discharge social as well as private responsibilities as members of the communities in which they operate."

As recently as 1978, the stockholders of IBM debated whether to eliminate charitable contributions as a matter of corporate policy. As you might gather from the ubiquitous IBM logo on public TV, the proposal was soundly defeated by more than fifty to one. But while the right of corporate giving has been duly secured, most businesses still do not respond to nonprofit appeals. In fact, only one in four businesses has even the most primitive giving program. In some rapid growth industries—oil, for example—the *percentage* of donations has actually decreased. And in many communities, corporate philanthropy boils down to three words: the United Way. Organizations not belonging to the federation—and that's most of us—can go fish.

The heralded "private sector initiatives" that were supposed to compensate for federal funding reductions under the Reagan administration simply never came to life. (We're reminded of the fraudulent promotion of California's Proposition 13, in which the huge property tax savings of major corporations were supposed to result in additional support for their nonprofit brethren. Out here in California, we're still waiting.) In fact, ever since the notion of an increased public role for private enterprise hit the public eye, business leaders have gone to great pains to point out not how much, but rather how little, they're willing to help.

And so we're left wondering: How realistic are our hopes for corporate support?

"As a publicly owned corporation," reads the Clorox Company's statement on corporate responsibility, [our] "first responsibility is to continue to build a sound, growing, profitable business. It must maximize the return on stockholders investment, it must provide quality products at a fair price, and it must provide rewarding jobs in a safe and clean workplace. Briefly, we must first do well as a Company before we can 'do good.'"

This statement might have been written by almost any corporation, though, in fact, Clorox enjoys something of an exemplary position within the world of corporate donors. The message must be understood by nonprofit fundraisers: Although many companies feel genuinely responsible to the communities in which they do business, they still have their own priorities, and the disinterested distribution of excess profits is not among them.

COURTING THE CORPORATE DOLLAR

So how can you ply your suit for the corporate donation? First, you should locate the most able and/or generous businesses in your community and head straight for their contributions officer or that newest kid on the philanthropic block, the corporate foundation.

In recent years, some of the largest and most active corporations have found it useful to set up in-house foundations to manage their grants and gifts. They often staff the foundations (though not always with someone who spends all of her time on contributions); and they take pains to establish application guidelines and criteria for evaluating proposals. You can approach the corporate foundation in almost the same way that you would approach a private foundation. In other words, find out what they fund, write a compelling proposal (the shorter, the better), and try to visit the foundation's officers or staff. While you're working on your proposal, you can keep these few subtle differences in mind:

• Corporations have two goals for their charitable dollars: *outreach* and *visibility*. Show the businessman how helping your organization will achieve this for *his company* and you'll be talking his language immediately.

• Businesses are almost fanatically interested in good management. No effort should be spared to assure them of the fiscal soundness of your group, and its administrative integrity.

• Corporate funders are even more wary of duplicating services; so if you're not unique, take pains to explain why you're still essential.

• Donors with limited experience tend to imitate one another. If other companies are backing your project, say so. Stress the level of support you receive from the community. Sometimes there will be one local funder—corporate, foundation, or even a government agency—which gives an unofficial seal of approval to a nonprofit's activities. And thus, the confidence for others to give.

Nine Tips for Avoiding the Mistakes That Everybody Else Will Make

1. Your organization must prove of *value* to the donor. That may be through improved employee relations, good press, programs named after the donor (always for a substantial price!), or any other means that might enhance their image in the community. Sometimes the quickest route to a corporation's pocketbook is through its employees. A number of corporations even have a gift program whereby they match, dollar for dollar, any charitable contributions made by the people who work for them.

2. Give the funder alternatives. It's often appealing to a corporate donor to be shown ways in which his gift can directly help to make more money for you. Sometimes, if you're trusted by the funder, you can suggest creative matching schemes, "challenge" grants, the underwriting of your annual benefit, seed funding of a new earned-income project, or other innovative methods. Corporations, for the most part, are new to the contributions game; their rules are still flexible.

3. Locate the people with the power. Remember that you're not dealing with the vast, amorphous, and ultimately impenetrable entity, "the corporation." Rather, you're dealing with a few individuals. Usually, one person. Sometimes the person in charge of corporate contributions can be located in marketing or public relations. Sometimes you'll deal directly with the CEO or an assistant vice-president. In any case, try to find out the aims, interests, and style of the decision-maker before you step into his office. Polish your case to a high gloss with this person in mind.

4. Research the local business world. Who are the movers and shakers? Who has a tradition of giving? Who, in fact, made any money last year so that they can afford to give?

5. Be prepared. Be punctual. Dress up. When you approach a potential business contributor you must present both a cogent explanation of the value of your work *and* a professional image. This is the wrong time to try educating the busi-

ness leader about alternative lifestyles. Donors need to feel confidence in their grantees. If you have another agenda with business, don't confuse it with getting money from them. And be positive! Speak about your accomplishments, goals, and the needs still left unfulfilled. Never resort to guilt-tripping the corporate funder because he makes money while the entire social service sector is suffering. Companies don't have to give their money away at all—and they certainly don't have to give it away to *you*.

6. Time your appeal. Corporations and even small businesses have peaks and valleys in their cash flow just as you do. Research can help you hit the right business at the right time. When you miss—and let's face it, this is a tough game—keep in touch and prepare for the next opportunity.

7. Use peer relationships. Rely on familiarity. You, no doubt, don't look, talk, or dress like the president of the vacuum cleaner company that you hope will give your group $10,000. As a result, you'll probably be met with some suspicion, perhaps the same kinds of feelings that you'll experience during your first interview at the corporate offices. To establish a successful relationship, this circle of mistrust must be interrupted. And it's up to you to do it. Enlist the appropriate Board members to solicit funds at corporate levels. Use the relationships that they have bred over the years. The strongest pitch will always come from a corporate peer who can vouch for your group's value and reliability. Better yet, someone who can say, "My company has already donated generously. Please join us."

8. Acknowledge generosity. Many corporate donors are motivated by the goodwill to be accrued in the community, so it's up to you to make certain that the community knows about your funder's gift. Naturally, most businesses believe that contributions to large organizations give them "more bang for the buck" in the outreach and visibility sweepstakes. That means you must be prepared at the time of solicitation to explain what kind of impact their gift will have on local problems, and how you plan to make their efforts known to the public. (Also,

be prepared for the occasional donor who wants to remain anonymous. Always, always, always ask before you make any public mention of a donor's gift.)

9. After you get a grant, take initiative. "My favorite organizations," asserts the contributions officer of an active multinational, "are the ones that make reports to me without having to be reminded. I once actually had to remind the largest agency in town to send me a letter acknowledging their grant so I could release it to them." The speaker, who is also a vice-president of marketing for her corporation, has more pressing job duties than giving money to the nonprofit sector. She appreciates the organizations that make life easier for her and, by extension, make her look good. Remember: After a business has given to you once and has felt no pain, you can often count on them for yearly contributions. Their gifts may follow with very little effort on your part other than absolute scrupulousness in reporting and proper acknowledgment.

Donations That Aren't Money: or Always Look a Gift Horse in the Mouth

"In-kind" gifts are what corporations may want to give you instead of cash. These "inventory" donations of supplies, equipment, services, and staff can sometimes prove more valuable than a check. Occasionally they will lead directly to future funding and the beginning of a beautiful relationship. Of course, the benefits for the corporation are obvious: They get to help you, accrue prestige, and take a tax write-off, all without actually spending a dollar.

From your point of view, in-kind gifts can be more problematic. Remember, a gift is only welcome if you can use it. The most desirable chronology is for a business to first make a cash donation; then, once you've established a relationship with the company, they may shower you with the equipment and services that you really need.

Supplies and Equipment: or Don't Accept a White Elephant Unless You're Soliciting for the Zoo

Of course there are some things everyone can use: type-writers, filing cabinets, desks, shelves, calculators. But other items—outmoded video equipment or the elderly computer—are worse than worthless. (Now *you'll* have to store or discard them.) Decide first what you need from a company. If they don't have it, be reluctant to take anything else. In this way you won't let them off the hook prematurely, nor will the donor come to believe that nonprofits are a dumping ground for the mistakes of the purchasing department. A good rule of thumb: Don't accept gifts that cost *you* money.

But you can also be creative about what you need. One dance company with a sense of humor choreographed a stunning performance piece, wrapping its dancers in hundreds of yards of plastic bubble packing material (that stuff no one can resist popping), all donated by the manufacturer.

Many cities have established corporate "equipment and supply banks," oftentimes run by the local United Way or another coordinating agency. Donations of consumable supplies, such as paper, envelopes, and ink are good possibilities. The best advice is to look at what you really need, and then figure out who has it. It may mean approaching a source you've never thought of before, or even a manufacturer in a distant city. The key, as always, will be to find the right person to ask, then speak to the aspects of your program that best fit the corporation's needs.

Services

Some corporations are generous with services to nonprofits. After all, their computers, addressing machines, mail sorters, copiers, and printing presses aren't (usually) busy twenty-four hours a day. These kinds of gifts can be very valuable indeed. But the rules that govern the selection of supplies and equipment apply equally to donated services, although nobody is going to try to "unload" services on you. Any donated labor is a genuine expenditure of time, money, and human effort. Don't waste it.

The best way to use donated services (mailing, printing, keypunching, or whatever) is to organize tasks well in advance so they can be done during the donor's slack time. Doing anything on a tight deadline, or which might require lots of last-minute changes or adjustments, is asking for trouble. You'll want to build a solid, trusting relationship with the corporate donor, and this is difficult if you're both frazzled with deadline pressure.

By now, the message should be clear: Know what you want, know when you have to have it, and then go to the company with a plan. Timetables and accurate deadlines are crucial. The last thing you want to do is disrupt your benefactor's business day. Also try to humanize the process. Whenever possible, deal directly with the people actually doing your work—the printers, typists, computer programmers, and their supervisors. These people are doing you an enormous favor. Make certain they know that you're grateful.

Staff

A popular variation on the theme of donated services is the loan of skilled business executives. Staff loans may take the form of an outright assignment on company time or merely be an encouragement to volunteer.

In either case, business volunteers in the past have mostly benefited the larger nonprofit agencies. Your challenge will be to show how skilled executives can substantially aid your effectiveness even though you're not the Red Cross or the Urban League. Many corporations that have not been forthcoming with cash may be more interested in this kind of assistance. In effect, your request acknowledges not merely their wealth, but their skill in acquiring it. And this strategy can be an indirect but speedier route to the corporate contributions officer.

Of course, volunteer contributions must be treated as seriously as money. Perhaps even more so, because the business volunteer serves as his corporation's eyes and ears; your organization is on display. Use a written agreement, with mutual responsibilities spelled out, and treat the entire operation in a polite, businesslike manner. Perhaps the best initial approach is to think in terms of short-term loans for limited projects. Typical use of business volunteers might include borrowing an accountant to help set up an improved bookkeeping system; or a public relations person to help launch a new project; or a CPA to audit your financial records.

Some cities have organized programs to match business executives with appropriate nonprofit agencies, such as the exemplary Business Volunteers for the Arts program, now in a number of cities. The local Chamber of Commerce is the place to seek information about such assistance.

The Last, Best Hope Is for the Future

Expectations about corporate donations have been unfairly raised by almost everyone. Duplicitous politicians, corporate executives pandering to antigovernment sentiment, and even naive but hopeful nonprofit workers have all contributed to the false promise that corporations will save our sector. But it's not going to happen. Even if corporate giving doubled over the next few years, it wouldn't begin to approach the amount donated by individuals, or the $40 billion cuts in federal social programs.

Philanthropy is a relatively new interest for most corporations. And in large measure, it's our task to help the most responsible corporate contributors spend their money wisely. The last few years have shown that many business leaders *are* interested in contributing to the communities in which they operate. With education, public awareness, and new centers of political power, we may find the corporate sector shouldering a fairer share of our society's social costs.

RAISING MONEY FROM INDIVIDUALS

We deserve some credit.

Individual donors—that's you, me, and our cousins in

Toledo—are responsible for 80 percent of our nation's charitable contributions. That's right, it's not the Ford Foundation, Citicorp, or even the Department of Health and Human Services that keeps the nonprofit sector running. It's ordinary people, chipping in the dimes and dollars, supporting the organizations that make a difference in our lives. In fact, individual giving delivers about seven times the combined gifts of all foundation and corporate funders—some $50 billion annually.

Admittedly, many of these dollars drop into the church collection plate on Sunday, or are otherwise pledged to religious causes. But the habit of personal generosity, inculcated throughout the centuries by organized religion, is now spreading to respond to a broader, more secular appeal. Once again, the smartest fundraisers will begin at home.

The Annual Fundraising Drive

The cornerstone of your campaign for individual donations is the annual fundraising drive. It can deliver dependable if modest sums on a predictable schedule, while keeping your name before the public, identifying prospects for major gifts, and setting the stage for more complicated and varied appeals to foundations, corporations, and the government. Every organization should have one. After all, nonprofit groups exist to serve the public; and a well-served public can be expected to reciprocate with financial support. Moreover, the annual fundraising drive helps answer the question most crucial to your life as a community organization: Is anybody out there really listening to us? Does anybody really care?

Seven Steps to a Sophisticated Yet Flexible Annual Drive

Step #1: Capture the Names.   The annual drive is a direct appeal to the people who care most about your existence. And who, you may (and should repeatedly) ask, might that be? Potentially, it's everyone who has ever crossed your doorstep.

Begin by collecting names and addresses: clients, students, neighbors, friends of your Board and staff, subscribers or audience members—everyone who knows your work. If you hold a benefit, keep a sign-up sheet at the door. Anytime anyone calls your office for information, get a name and address.

But don't stop there. Sit down with your Board, staff, and volunteers, the inner circle of your organization, and brainstorm more names. To whom are you important? Who owes you favors? What characteristics do your current supporters share and where can you find others like them? Borrow names from other organizations. (Many groups publicize their donors' names as a way of honoring their gifts. You can look up their addresses in the phone book and add them to your own list of budding prospects.) Building the roster of potential donors is a year-round job. Names should pump through the organization like oil through the well-maintained automobile.

Step #2: Categorize the Names. A large stack of undifferentiated names won't help much. Now you must search for clues that will tell you why people might *want* to give to your group. On a set of 5 × 7 index cards, record your prospects':
- Name and address (zip code is essential)
- Telephone number (if you don't have it, look it up!)
- Occupation, if known
- Any affiliation with your group

Systematize the cards. Some organizations have different file boxes listing donors by size of gift, date of gift, and contact person. Experiment with color coding: blue for clients, pink for friends of Board members, yellow for people who attended your benefit, etc. The coded cards will enable you to select different categories of prospects for various mailings, and then monitor their performance. The most important aspect of any system is that it work for you. The annual campaign grows over the years by successful experimentation. Your task is to balance the combination of sure bets with uncertain but promising prospects for the future.

Step #3: Time It Right. Now you're holding a good list. In direct mail jargon, you've combined "hot" prospects (your own people) and "warm" prospects (people without a direct connection, but some natural sympathy to your goals). So when do you make the appeal?

Market research has shown that fall is the best and summer the worst time to approach the public. However, you'll need to keep an ear to your organization's heartbeat to determine the timing. When is the cash flow at its lowest ebb? When is the greatest need for working capital? Is there a particular time of year when you are in the news? (For example, an environmental agency's fund drive will have greater impact if it coincides with its annual Clean Air Assessment). If you can't time your drive around a genuine publicity event, then at least try to place feature stories in the local media that will enhance your group's public recognition.

As soon as you've decided when to begin the drive, gather a committee—led by a staff person, but involving Board members—to organize and oversee the project. Together you'll:

• Set a date for the mailing to go out

• Develop a time-line for assembling and printing the necessary pieces to be included in the mailing

• Recruit volunteers to collate materials, stuff envelopes, and handle bulk mailing; or, alternately, decide to contract out these services

• Construct a budget for the mailing, based on the figure that the Board and staff have determined

Step #4: Feed the Envelope. This is the heart of your pitch. When the prospect opens your legal-size envelope, he should encounter an attractive, coordinated package with highly visual appeal. It should contain the following:

1. A cover letter
2. Your brochure
3. One other informational piece
4. A donor response card
5. A return envelope

The cover letter: Aim for a personal touch from the beginning. On organizational letterhead, compose one or two pages that convey the vigorous concern of a well-loved, though respectfully distant, relative. If possible, use word processing to individuate each salutation: "Dear Mrs. Golden" is always preferable to "Dear Friend." Your tone should be sincere ("Let me assure you of how important we consider your support"), direct ("We need your money"), and upbeat ("You can make a difference!"). The signature at the bottom should belong to the president of your Board.

You may need several versions of the letter to send to the various segments of your prospect list. (The letter mailed to your students' parents may not be appropriate for public officials or audience members.) The most efficient way to do this is to use interchangeable first paragraphs: "As a parent, you'll appreciate the fact that . . ." "As someone who's used our telephone referral service . . ." "As someone doing business in our community. . . ."

The body of the letter only requires two versions: one for people who are at least casually familiar with your work (even if they've never given you money), and one for prospects who know practically nothing about your organization. Much of the two letters will be identical, and drawn directly from your fundraising case statement. If there's a cardinal rule here, it's this: Never bore the reader. That means throttle the jargon, store the platitudes, and reduce your prose to a few well-selected anecdotes and assertions that prove your worth and identify your organization as a good risk for a donation. And be sure to tell the potential donor what she'll get for her money—a subscription to your newsletter, a gift, free tickets, etc.

Your organizational brochure: The brochure—a three-fold, single sheet brightened by compelling photographs and clever graphics—is your quick introduction for the people who won't thoroughly read your letter. And that's almost everybody. (Now you know why it's important to have a brochure that fits into a legal-size envelope! See Chapter 9.)

One other informational piece: This piece is not essential, and it's better to leave it out than to put in something questionable. However, an excellent newspaper feature, a winning testimonial from a renowned (or at least popular) public figure, or an information sheet clearly stating your case and cause can all add another dimension to your appeal.

A donor card listing categories of giving and premiums: The purpose of the donor card is to assure the prospect that (1) you're not going to lose his donation, (2) you're going to send him whatever premium you've promised (or at least a thank-you letter), and (3) that he really does understand what it is he's signing up for.

The card can consist of one simple line like, "Here's my membership check for $25 to support your important work," with space for name, address, and phone number. Or the card might feature a list of membership categories from "Sponsor" through "Donor" to "Patron" with different privileges tied to each giving level. ("A $25 donation entitles you to two free tickets to a show of your choice; for $35, we make certain only short people sit in front of you; for $100, we pretend that you wrote the play.") The donor cards should look professional, businesslike, and inviting. They should also be *easy to use.* In the best of all possible worlds, the prospect will read your materials, sign the donor card, and expeditiously drop a check into the return envelope. He shouldn't have to work to make a contribution.

The return envelope: Be sure it's large enough to hold the donor card and a check, and small enough to fit into the mailing envelope without folding. Your organization's address should be printed on the outside. *You'll* provide the postage. Use a return-postage-paid envelope if you can afford it; it will cost you more, but most experts agree it's worth it. Many donors, despite their best intentions to support you, will be defeated by the weighty task of finding a postage stamp. Don't give them the excuse.

The envelope that contains all this should be legal-size; of good quality; printed with your organization's name, address, and logo; and hand-addressed or typed. If your mailing is absolutely immense, or volunteers are nil, then consider having the envelopes professionally rototyped, a method of mass addressing that appears hand-typed. The least desirable alternative is a mailing label. To most people the label shouts MASS MAILING—DO NOT TAKE SERIOUSLY! The more personal your solicitation looks, the better its reception. Of course it's essential to have the correct name and address.

Use a stamp if possible. (That is, if you have plenty of volunteers to help with the licking.) Even if you're mailing bulk rate (and of course, you should), ask the post office about individual bulk postage stamps. Although they increase the mailing workload, they improve your chances of getting past the wary eye of the homeowner purging his metered junk mail.

Step #5: Don't Mail It Yet! After you've piled your letters in neat, abundant stacks, placed your return envelopes beside them, printed a sufficient number of brochures, and all seems to be ready—*stop and proofread everything one more time*. Nothing is so horrible as to send out a direct mail piece containing typos. Or worse, downright inaccuracies. (Our favorite gaffe had a local politician promising to "minimize the use of your tax dollars" when he meant quite the opposite. To make certain everyone saw the error, his staff then crossed out the offensive verb and substituted "maximize." Remarkably, he still won. You may not. Check and check again!)

And last, a personal note at the bottom of the letter ("Thanks for all your past support. Sincerely, Jim Fundraiser") takes very little time and carries a great payoff. Frank Oppenheimer, founder and director of San Francisco's famous EXPLORATORIUM science museum, wrote hundreds of these little notes each year on membership renewal letters. His approach was hard to resist as evidenced by an enviably high renewal rate.

Step #6: Throw a Mailing Party. As you undoubtedly know by now, your organization can send mail bulk rate. This designation refers to the U.S. Postal Service scheme to give nonprofit groups a break on postage in exchange for our doing an incredible amount of extra work—sorting, coding, wrapping up bundles with string or rubber bands, affixing colored stickers. These are the skills you'd use to run a small assembly line factory. And, in fact, that's exactly what you'll be doing. You can apply for a bulk permit at a locally designated post office. The permit must be renewed yearly. *Do not neglect to do this.* Although the bulk rate postage cost is not as cheap as it should be, or as cheap as it used to be, it's still a considerable savings over first class, and worth the trouble *if* you plan carefully and have plenty of lead time.

Every nonprofit organization should cultivate friends at the local post office. The regulations governing the bulk rate permit are formidable and constantly in revision; it's necessary for at least one person on the mailing committee to know them cold and assume responsibility for actually getting the mailing out. Dropping a 5,000-piece mailing on an unprepared and unfriendly post office is roughly the equivalent of sealing it up in bottles and tossing it out to sea. Everyone has a favorite horror story of mailings arriving months late and mangled, or never arriving at all. A large West Coast nonprofit, thoroughly experienced in fundraising, was forced to cancel a $100,000 benefit when its invitations were discovered, two weeks before the event, in a cobwebbed corner of the bulk mail center.

. Post office personnel have a lot of discretion in the timing of bulk mail. The designation does not indicate the same urgency as first class, and many postal workers consider it a colossal headache. Just the same, you're dealing here with hardworking people who will respond to your requirements like friendly professionals if you take their needs into account. And, of course, when a mailing gets into the hands of your public in a particularly efficient manner, thank the people who were responsible. A novel idea, you think? Perhaps, and the postal workers will probably think so too, since the usual public response is either indifference or criticism. That will make your courtesy stand out all the more.

Step #7: Don't Stop Now! Do not sit back and wait for the money to roll in. Now is the time to follow up on your mailing with a telephone campaign. (Hmm . . . This is more work than you first thought, isn't it?) Just remember that your annual drive happens but once a year. Do it right, and read on.

The Telephone Connection: Yet Another Step-by-Step Guide to Success

Now that you've invested heart, soul, hours, and dollars in your annual drive, you'll need to go one step better: Sit down, pick up the receiver, and ask face-to-phone for the money. It'll make all the difference in the world. (Some groups report tripling their response with a telephone follow-up.) Consider it an investment in future giving. Most of your energy will be spent on the first-time donor; and with each succeeding year, you'll meet less resistance.

The telephone follow-up should occur no more than a week after your mailing has been received. How can you possibly time the course of the U.S. mail? The best way is to riddle your list with "ringers"—staff and Board members or friends who live within the targeted zip code areas.

The phone campaign itself requires the same kind of organization that made a success of the mailing. You'll need someone to coordinate tasks, schedule volunteers, and provide the equipment, moral support, and good humor. If the mailing organizer is still standing and willing to take this one on, too, all the better. If no one in the organization has ever done a phone campaign, don't despair. You can learn the intricacies of holding a phonathon by volunteering to work on a more experienced group's campaign. Surely there's another worthy nonprofit in town that you can help for an evening or two?

Step #1: Tools. You'll need a reasonable number of telephones and phone lines—at least three or four. If your office can't handle the load, latch on to space from a well-connected Board member. Think twice about renting more phones; it's expensive, and you'll be tempted not to rip them back out when you're done. When in doubt, borrow.

Step #2: Tactics. Not surprisingly, the people who best know your organization make the most capable solicitors, although anyone can be trained to do it. (Some organizations even hire outside hands, paying them by the hour.) In any case, the person on your end of the line should be familiar with your organization, knowledgeable about donor categories and premiums, and capable of handling any "hard questions" people might ask. The smartest tactic is to have volunteers describe why *they personally* support your organization. ("Because I'm getting paid to do it" is never the right answer.) Phoners should have donor cards in front of them when they make calls so that information about previous gifts and any special interests of the prospect is immediately available for reference. This information should be carefully screened. Little can equal the embarrassment of the freshly recruited volunteer who calls a longtime supporter and big contributor and innocently asks her if she plans to subscribe.

Step #3: The Script. Volunteers are understandably nervous about the thought of calling strangers and asking them for money. Such a speech combines two of the biggest social taboos in Western society. But your callers will feel noticeably better with a smart script in front of them. And in no time, they'll improve upon your efforts, chewing over your words until they're comfortable. (A solicitor for a major opera company started his pitches with, "Now let me be perfectly frank with you. . . ." No one could figure out what it was about the opera membership drive that necessitated such great candor; nevertheless, the volunteer scored an enviable subscription record.) In any case, your script provides the departure point even for the most confident, golden-throated caller. Typically, the script will tell the solicitor:

• Introduce yourself and your organization, and ask if you're calling at a convenient time. Mention that you'll only take a few minutes.

• Ask if the mailing was received and if you can answer any questions.

• Tell the prospect exactly what you'd like her to do:
    —renew her membership, or
    —increase her donation, or
    —make a special gift

• Ask the prospective donor for a specified amount. Respond politely to no, enthusiastically to yes; and thank her for her time.

• Record the information on the donor card for future reference.

The conversation might run something like this:

"Hello, is this Ms. Previous Donor? Good evening, Ms. Donor, I'm Jane Volunteer, with the Save the Blue Nurd Campaign. Do you have a minute? We're calling this evening to follow up our mailing of last week to see if you received it and to answer any questions you may have. Did you receive our information?"

"Well, I think I might have—we get so much of that kind of thing . . ."

"We know that, Ms. Donor. And that's why we're calling—so that you can see why the Blue Nurd campaign stands out a little from the others. Did you know that Blue Nurd breeding grounds in the South Pacific have been virtually wiped out by oil spills over the last few years? One of our most important projects is to clean up a ten-square-mile area in the Pacific and get these beautiful creatures breeding again."

"Well, that does seem important."

"It really is—we can't afford to lose any more Nurds. You'll be glad to know that thanks to the pledges we received last year from you and other concerned people, we were able to save more than two hundred Nurds from certain extinction. May I put you down this year for a $25 membership?"

"Well, I'll consider it. Your work is very important."

"Thank you so much. It's concerned people like you that keep us going."

Then make a note on the donor card, so that you can follow up. Some organizations like to immediately put another pledge envelope in the mail to Ms. Donor, with a little note: "Good to talk to you last night. Thanks for your help. (signed) Jane." This is a great tactic, worth the time and money.

Step #4: Training. Now you're all set, except for one trifling matter. Your volunteer caller is scared. He's scared that people will be rude and yell at him for disturbing their dinner. He's scared that they will ridicule his devotion to the Blue Nurd. But most of all, he's scared they'll say "NO!"

It is essential to deal with this fear during the training process. Once out in the open, it can be exposed for the weak and puny thing it is. As long as it lies hidden away, it remains a cold fist around the hearts of your able volunteers. "All right," you say cheerily, "what if someone does say no? What can happen?" Get people to talk about it. Exorcise the ghost of "hearing no." Soon people will realize that someone saying no is simply someone saying no. People are almost never rude, they simply say, "I'm not interested tonight," and hang up. But what if they say: "No, you disgusting pervert. And don't ever call me again or I'll call the police!"? First of all, this practically never happens. But even if it does, so what? So you've reached a crazy person. Simply say "Sorry to have bothered you." Hang up. And then make a note on the donor card. In fact, you'd better pull the donor card—and go on to the next call.

A final caveat about telephone soliciting: This method has become so prevalent in some locales that it has become a nuisance. (Those offensive recorded messages from politicians around election time can turn off even the most partisan supporter.) If you live in an area that suffers from over-solicitation, stick very close to your own members and friends with your telephone follow-up. Or at least be prepared for the occasional irate prospect.

Step #5: Expanding Your Grasp. Although a phone campaign should almost always be used in conjunction with a membership drive, there are other occasions when it is also warranted:

• When you have a crisis. Your building has burned to the ground. You've lost your lease. Your office has been swept away in the flood. People respond with wonderful generosity to such emergencies. (A small professional theater company, the victim of arson, recently raised $20,000 in donations and loans in two days.) But don't cry wolf. Emergency telephone fundraising is not the appropriate solution to abrupt cash flow problems. Your monthly scramble to meet payroll and failure to predict the loss of an important government contract are poor reasons for crisis fundraising.

• When you have an important, emergency issue. Letters need to be written to legislators about a pending bill; bodies need to be mustered to pack a community meeting; a whole neighborhood needs to be informed of a disastrous decision by the zoning board.

• When you're holding a benefit

• When you have an issue with particularly broad appeal, which reaches out of your usual area of service

Finally, after you've got a good solid annual mail campaign running smoothly, you may be tempted to branch out. You'll want to collect some new names, constructing a cool or even cold list; you can even arrange to rent or trade lists with other organizations. Direct mail solicitation has made fortunes, particularly in politics. Everybody in your organization probably has a favorite anecdote about some struggling organization that raised a quarter-million through the mail in six months. What may not be recalled so readily are the numerous stories wherein organizations lose their shirts, or the sobering fact that it cost $245,000 to raise the $250,000. But by all means, talk to as many people as possible who have journeyed the route of the cold list; learn from their experience. And if after consultation you think there's a good chance for success, take the plunge with the help of enthusiastic Board members or volunteers. Give them their heads to do the research and put together a plan and budget. (Mailing lists rented from various services usually have a 5,000-name minimum order and will probably cost at least $1 a name.) Once you've got the facts and figures straight away on paper, look them over hard. Cold direct mailings seldom earn better than a 1-3 percent return the first time. If that makes sense for your organization—to expand a donor base in a particular zip code, or because a recent windfall of good publicity has made your name recognized with a specific constituency—then you might consider the gamble as though you were entering into a new, limited, but costly small business.

The Great Leap Forward: Major Donors

With a solid annual drive in place, the fundraiser turns her attention to cultivating the rare orchids of the contributions garden, the Major Donors. The idea of major donors has undeniable appeal. As the story goes, it's easier to solicit five $1,000 contributions than to find one thousand $5 contributions. Right and wrong. In most organizations both levels of giving are necessary. The standard rule of thumb is the 80/20 principle: 80 percent of the money comes from 20 percent of the contributors.

The most important characteristic of a major donor is not how much money he has, but how much he's willing to give to *you*. And the definition of a major donor is largely determined by your current level of donations. If $50 is the largest donation you've ever received from an individual, then that individual becomes your first major donor. This person is sure to have like-minded friends and colleagues, and they may well be the next to be drawn into your fold.

Of course, the key is forethought. Each potential major donor is meticulously (but discreetly) researched as to his interests, affiliations, and ability to give. The very best person to approach the potential major donor is a peer, colleague, or friend. If none of these valuable allies are available, you'll have to rely upon an articulate and knowledgeable Board

member. If you're new at this game, then you might send two
people to make the appeal. (But never more than two. You
don't want to intimidate.) Both of your solicitors aren't likely
to clutch up at the same moment.

Contrary to popular wisdom, one need not have an unlimited expense account to attract major donors. Most people
with the necessary commitment and disposable income are not
particularly interested in being wined and dined by the representatives of a struggling nonprofit organization. In a one-on-
one situation, a simple lunch or coffee date is appropriate.

"Fine," you say, "there she sits hovering over the tuna
salad. Now how do I get her to pull out her check book?"
Here's one scenario that's worked for thousands:

1. Start by behaving like a good host: Make family inquir-
ies, or whatever will put your guest at ease. ("Thank good-
ness," she'll think, "I'm not going to be hustled by some hard
sell artist.") This conversation is *not* manipulation, it is your
genuine attempt to let the potential donor know she's seen as
a person, not just a name on your file card.

2. Ease into talking about the organization. Maybe you
can share a piece of good news—word of a new project or new
employee, encouraging enrollment statistics that are just
about to be made public. (If your organization has any really
bad news waiting in the wings, this is probably the wrong
time to solicit new major donors. If you tell the donor, she's
not likely to contribute; if you don't tell her, she'll feel burned
and angry when she finds out.) Provide ample detail about any
projects that particularly interest your prospect. And stress
how her gift can make a real difference in your work.

3. Ask if she has any questions. Listen very carefully to
her concerns, and answer in a straightforward manner. If she
raises issues beyond your knowledge, promise to get back
later with the answers. And then do it!

4. If you're soliciting as a team, decide in advance which
one of you will *ask for a donation*. Based upon your knowledge of the donor's interests, ask for a specific sum for a specific purpose. *Then be quiet!*

You: "I can tell from our conversation that you understand how important our work is, and how much it means to the community. I would like you to consider making a contribution of $500 toward our campership program for boys from low-income families." (Pass a pledge card across the table.)

The result will be *silence*. And you'll want to fill up this space with idle chatter. Don't. You'd probably find yourself saying things like, "But, of course, if that's too much, we can use anything you can give us . . ." or equally clumsy and self-defeating equivocations. Just sit tight. Try not to look as if you're waiting for the jury's verdict in a homicide trial, and resist the urge to shred your napkin.

Prospect: "Well, I'm not sure if right at this time . . . I have some major expenses this month, and . . ."

You: "I understand, of course. We'd be glad to accept your pledge and a date you'd find convenient. Or we could bill you monthly for five months, starting next month if you wish. That way there won't be such an impact all at once."

5. Try to come away with something concrete. A check is the grand prize, of course. Next best is a signed pledge card. But if the prospect only promises to think about it, that's fine too. In this case, agree upon a date when you'll get back to her about her decision. ("Thanks so much for meeting with us. We'll get back to you in about ten days. In the meantime, I'll send you the clippings on our community garden project.") Then follow up immediately with a thank-you note and any material you've promised.

Variations on this scenario may also be used to solicit *groups* of potential major donors. Occasions such as a luncheon given by a well-known Board member, a reception, or an organizational open house are all good opportunities for recruiting major donors, if you've planned ahead. These parties should be thought of as educational opportunities as well as tools for raising money. Engage one or two people to make a presentation and answer any questions that might come up. But don't forget, people are also there to have *fun*.

Somewhere deep into the presentation, you can make

your request for funds. While the guests are pondering their commitments and bank balances, show your slides, offer a brief testimonial from a client, or simply pass the canapes. Then wrap up by thanking everyone and collecting pledge cards. Strange as it may seem, the essential step of *asking for the money* is sometimes not taken at these gatherings. A Board member of an otherwise sophisticated community organization told us, "The open house went so well and everyone was having such a good time, we just didn't have the heart to ask them to donate."

This illustrates one of the worst mistakes of novice fundraisers: believing that it's somehow impolite to ask for money from people you're entertaining, or that asking for money will spoil a good time. You need not—should not— employ strong-arm tactics, or any sort of guilt-inducing behavior. Yet people don't give unless they're asked. They will eat your hors d'oeuvres until the cows come home and never put pen to check unless you clearly and directly ask them to do so.

A Word About the Magic Words: Thank You

Whenever you receive a donation—membership, subscription, pledge, whatever—*immediately thank the donor and do it in writing*.

An ordinary membership renewal can be handled with a cordial postcard. But anything truly outstanding—a donor who's elevated his status from "Member" to "Benefactor," a first-time donation, an extra-large check—deserves an immediate, personalized response. Today the convenience of word processing allows each of us to pretend that the Publisher's Clearing House Sweepstakes is writing directly to us and us alone. Short of such marvels, you can't go wrong with a hand-written note at the bottom of your standard form thank-you letter. (It might read: "Thanks so much for increasing your pledge. I'm enclosing an advance copy of our next newsletter with a story about our Meals for Seniors program. Best, Steve Board.") The donor who is made to feel unique and important is the donor who will give again, possibly at an increased level.

To drive home this important point, let's look at two organizations that grappled, one successfully, one not so well, with those powerfully simple words.

Our first group is a social action agency working on issues of particular interest to women and girls. Their fundraising membership base is broad; many of their supporters give as little as $5. One day this organization persuaded a well-known author to host a luncheon for some prospective donors in the literary field. One of the author's friends, Ms. Likely Prospect, attended and was very impressed with what she heard about the good work of the organization. She thought she'd found her cause. She went right home and wrote out a check for $100 and enclosed it with a letter to the director of the organization, whom she'd met at the lunch. She wrote about how moved she'd been by the group's work and said she'd like to get involved, particularly in any projects they might have involving women writers and their struggles for recognition. As Ms. Prospect was respected in the literary world, her offer should have been taken to heart. But sad to say, it was not. Not only did Ms. Prospect get no follow-up on her offered help, she received an ugly form letter, with her name misspelled, telling her what wonderful work the organization did, and only incidentally thanking her for her check. Need we say that Ms. Likely Prospect is likely to remain a one-time donor to the organization?

In another city, there was an organization that put out a magazine dedicated to investigative reporting on issues of social justice and politics. It had international distribution, a good advertising base, and a slick format. It also had a vast direct mail network and depended on extra contributions above the subscription price to survive. For all its appearance of success, the magazine was as precarious as any other nonprofit organization. One day a check for $100 came into the magazine's office in response to a pledge drive, with a scrawled note: "Let me know if you ever need a loan." Now $100 was not a particularly large pledge for this group, but the canny direct mail fundraiser recognized the signs of a "hot prospect":

• The check was a first time donation for an unusually high amount.

• The donor suggested openness to further involvement.

The development director immediately dashed off a letter of profuse thanks that spelled out how the organization's interests and the donor's might very well be the same. She asked the donor to call her personally if he was ever in town. Months went by. And then the donor called with an offer: He would set up a revolving loan fund for the organization with $10,000. This fund could be used like a line of credit to ease the group's cash flow problems, particularly when they needed front money to finance a direct mail campaign. As it happened, the donor had just made a fortune speculating in silver futures and was looking for someone to help. He'd made donations to a number of organizations whose work he liked, but the magazine's fundraiser was the first one to make him feel that his pledge really *made a difference*.

Donors are looking for personal impact and personal recognition in return for their money. For *any* contribution or offer that is at all special, a word of personal thanks is important. In fact, its importance cannot be overstressed.

THE REST OF THE BALL OF WAX

Filling in the interstices of the fundraising plan are all the garage sales, raffles, clambakes, benefit concerts, bingo parlors, auctions, celebrity softball games, candy bar sales, casino nights, theater parties, ad books, penny carnivals, and so on and on ad infinitum, some might say, ad nauseum.

They sound so simple, fun, and carefree. They aren't. Each and every one of these light-hearted activities requires the same meticulous planning, budgeting, publicizing, and follow-up that you give to every other aspect of your programming and fundraising. To do anything less is to guarantee failure. And nothing can burn out good volunteers more quickly than a fundraiser that goes bust. The words most frequently heard following a fundraiser are, "We all had a good time, but we didn't make any money."

At the risk of sounding unduly negative, our best advice on special event fundraisers is a series of Don'ts:

• Don't do them unless people in the organization are really excited and *committed to selling tickets.* Thrusting one of these activities on a reluctant organization is a recipe for frustration.

• Don't do them unless you have a reasonable expectation of making a considerable amount of money. All these special events are labor-intensive. It doesn't make sense to labor for weeks in order to make $200.

• Don't do them unless you have the person-power to pull them off without undue strain on the staff.

• Don't do them if your fallback rationale is "Well, at least it'll be good public relations." Public relations are important, but the first duty of a fundraising activity is to raise money.

• Don't do them unless you have absolutely minimized your cash costs. The most successful special event fundraisers get everything from the hall to the crepe paper donated.

• Don't assume that because an activity is easy, it is also cheap; don't assume that because an activity is cheap, it is also easy.

We must also say that a beautifully organized, well-attended, and financially lucrative special event is a genuine high for the organization. And with imagination, energy, and resolve it can turn into an *annual* gold-mine.

If you do have an enthusiastic group of people willing to work on a special event or grass roots fundraiser, then by all means—bring on the bingo, baked goods, band, candy, and balloons!

Fundraising in a Crisis

We'd all prefer to fundraise from a position of strength; no one chooses to fundraise in a crisis. But in the life of each organization there will be times when you are pushed to the wall and must come up with a sizeable sum *or else.*

In these cases it is always better to do something rather than nothing (which is, of course, guaranteed to raise *no* money). And it's usually better to return to the familiar tools, rather than begin to explore new methods. Thus, a crisis is the right time to go to trusted friends of the organization and hit them up once again. It is the right time to ask someone to throw a benefit *for* you. (It's the wrong time to hold your first dinner dance and fashion show—particularly without underwriting.) It is the right time to go through all your tried and true fundraising moves on an accelerated schedule with all the heart you can muster. It is also the right time to crank up a public relations effort. Seed the press with articles about your value and critical needs.

The most dangerous aspect of a financial crisis is the way it can paralyze the people laboring within the organization. The crisis will almost always be temporary, but the loss of nerve could be permanent. And that kind of spiritual bankruptcy can be as deadly as the red ink in your balance statement.

ADDITIONAL RESOURCES

Tested Ways to Successful Fund Raising by George A. Brakeley, Jr. Amacom (a division of American Management Associations), 135 West 50th Street, New York, NY 10020.

This is a classic in the field. The book was written for larger organizations, but it outlines proven methods that can be adapted for groups of any size.

Grassroots Fundraising Journal, P.O. Box 14754, San Francisco, CA 94114.

In this context, "grassroots" refers to organizations that are strongly rooted in their communities. This bimonthly publication provides great tips and keen analysis for organizations serious about making the proper connections between fundraising and their constituencies.

The Grassroots Fundraising Book by Joan Flanagan. The Youth Project, 1555 Connecticut Avenue, N.W., Washington, D.C. 20036.

Joan Flanagan's book is the definitive resource for special events.

7

****

HOW TO GET A GRANT

A short course in research, writing, and tying up loose ends

There is a certain Buddhistic calm that comes from having . . . money in the bank. —*Tom Robbins*

The idea of applying for a grant probably occurred early in the life of your nonprofit organization.

This is the way it usually begins. . . .

You belong to a small group of people with a vision who have already made something happen. Perhaps you've opened a child care referral service using home telephones; or you've joined a community chorus bravely staging its first *Messiah;* or you've convinced the local clinic to hire a bilingual doctor. You've tasted success. Everyone feels invigorated and ready for the next challenge.

All you need is more money. In short, *a grant.*

EVERYBODY KNOWS WHAT A GRANT IS, RIGHT?

For our purposes, a grant is a sum of money awarded by some outside agency to a nonprofit organization, which enables it to perform a specific function or service.

Grants vary enormously in size and purpose. They cover everything from a family foundation's $100 United Way pledge to the federal government's $2,500,000 award for constructing a drug abuse treatment center. The people responsible for giving away the money may be your neighbors or anonymous government bureaucrats. They may be keenly interested, even meddlesome, or steadfastly indifferent to your project's ultimate success or failure. Yet despite these differences, there are several characteristics that typify almost any grant.

• Formal applications. Grant-making agencies generally require a detailed account of the work you propose to accomplish. You can choose to make your application succinct and informative; or you can burden everybody concerned with unnecessary information and inflated prose.

• Limited scope and duration. Grant projects have a beginning and an end. Their results are measurable, their goals realistic. Global problems, such as the eradication of hunger, disease, and ignorance, are the concern and inspiration for entire organizations, not the meat and potatoes of individual grants. At best, grant projects represent one small step for mankind—though perhaps an ambitious leap forward for an organization. They are also limited in duration. Generally, grants cover a single year, though they may be renewable for several more. The point here is that grants ultimately prove to be undependable. Like all good things, they come to an end.

• Accountability. A grant may take the form of a gift, but it is not the pot of gold at the end of the rainbow to spend as your whims might dictate. Rather, you use a grant application to propose a specific project or action. If you're skillful (and lucky), the funder hands over the money, and eventually wants to hear about the results. You may be asked to forward a single-page evaluation at the end of the grant year; or you might find yourself ploughing through a maze of federal reporting requirements, wondering why you took the money in the first place. In any case, you have a moral and legal obligation to fulfill the terms of your grant, or to give the money back.

Experienced proposal writers might add the following observations.

• No matter how much a funder decides to give you, it

will almost always be less than you wanted, needed, or asked
for.

• Every gift has its price. Grants usually arrive with some
kind of strings attached, and you must decide if they'll bind or
strangle your project.

• Finally, although you can apply your sharpest skills and
best connections in pursuit of any funding source, you'll seldom *really* know why you were successful one time and failed
the next.

All of this leads us to the mystique of the grant writer. In
your mind's eye, you've probably seen him at work. He's
sealed away with his office typewriter, downing cups of black
coffee, racing against a deadline. What alchemy he works—
wielding arcane terminology, juggling numbers and formulae
to turn the most leaden project into gold. It's all so mysterious. You'll never be able to do it.

We're here to say it isn't so.

Grant writing is an exercise in logical thought and clear
language. It's a skill that needs to be mastered by every nonprofit administrator. And it's essential because numerous
granting agencies, despite somewhat exaggerated reports of
their demise, are still alive and kicking.

WHO FUNDS WHAT AND WHY

Today in America, there are four major sources of funding for
nonprofit groups: government agencies, foundations, corporations, and individual donors. It is the first two sources which
use the grant process. (See Chapter 6 for more information on
corporate and individual fundraising.)

Government Agencies

Over the past three decades, government at all levels has expanded its partnership with independent nonprofit agencies to
support a staggering array of projects. More than 40,000 governmental entities across the nation now fund everything from
the study of anorexia nervosa to the improvement of municipal

zoos; from traditional health care to the hospice movement; from averting warfare to planning the holocaust. The federal government alone boasts more than 1,400 domestic assistance programs, granting billions of dollars annually to nonprofit organizations of nearly every imaginable stripe. A survey by the Urban Institute's Non-Profit Sector Project found that in the early 1980s government support at all levels constituted 40 percent of nonprofit revenues.

How does this square with the story what we all know only too well: the pervasive and devastating federal cutbacks? To answer that question, we must enter the world of political process, a world not notably susceptible to logic.

The priorities of government funding, be it federal, state, or local, are set in the hurly-burly of the political arena. Here we find ample room for selfless aspirations, political posturing, or simply good intentions gone awry. (One thinks of Lyndon Johnson's Great Society as the classic example of all three conditions—the final epitaph for its most ambitious project being, "The War on Poverty: Declared but Never Fought.") In the volatile life of government, today's pressing needs are tomorrow's boondoggles. Accountability, cost-effectiveness, and results are all too often honored in the breach and pushed aside for the snappy slogan and good press. "We said that we would reduce poverty immeasurably," ran the old joke at the Office of Economic Opportunity. "And in fact, everything we tried was immeasurable."

In 1972, the federal government under the Nixon administration began to reshape its grant-making mechanism under the rubric of the New Federalism. Basically, this called for the relegation of decision-making authority to local government. From the beginning, the New Federalism was promoted in the name of community control. Unfortunately, it has often simply meant cutbacks, and less access to power by community groups.

But of course, the real reductions did not arrive until the presidential election of 1980 and the advent of the Reagan administration, which cut through social programs with the delicacy of a meat ax. Nonprofit organizations howled. Their constituencies formed lobbies and pressure groups. And still, according to the Urban Institute, over half the groups funded by the government experienced reductions over a two-year period, with another 35 percent receiving no customary increase for inflation. And the picture continues to darken.

What does all this bode for the future of government funding? There is no doubt that the salad days of federal grants are over. But by the first law of politics—survival—we can expect to see our federal, state, and local representatives continue to respond to human needs as they are signaled by well-orchestrated outrage and votes. And nonprofit groups will no doubt continue to reap some of the benefits of government largess. On a somewhat more optimistic note, there is even good reason to suspect that a few aspects of the partnership between state and independent agencies, such as contracting out for municipal services, will keep growing because of the fiscal advantages for all concerned.

Stalking the Government Grant

Today is not the best day to start looking for tax-supported funding. In fact, it seems irresponsible to encourage any organization to invest much time seeking government grants if it has not already received some degree of support. The fact remains that most groups now funded are themselves engaged in the all-out defense of what they have scraped together over the years.

With this somewhat gloomy introduction, we can only offer a few suggestions to those who would persevere in the face of somewhat daunting odds.

1. Position yourself for greater access to new sources. Start at the local level. Ask your elected officials to help you locate new funding programs. Pay particular attention to community development block grants, economic development block grants, redevelopment funds, and rural assistance programs. As federal programs decentralize, these revenue-sharing allocations receive more money at the local level. They may prove susceptible to your good reputation and—more likely—the suggestions of your influential friends.

Keep in mind that this kind of effort also introduces your organization as a dynamic quantity to local politicians and their aides. You should get to know these people; eventually you'll be asking them for favors. And remember that, in many cases, the outcome of a grant proposal is determined as much by the quality of the lobbying as the quality of the project. (See Chapter 10.)

2. Do your homework. We're talking here about research. You should become familiar with several useful tools, each available at your public library. They include:

• *The Catalog of Federal Domestic Assistance*—covers listings for more than one thousand grant programs, complete with objectives of each program, eligibility requirements, application procedures, and awards range. Since this information dates very quickly, you can use the catalog most efficiently to locate regional contact offices, which may then provide current information. Your aim is to identify people who can directly affect the decision-making process. And your approach should be warm, cordial, and unyielding in the face of rebuffs.

• *The Federal Register*—publishes the daily record of the House and Senate, including regulations, changes, and allocations for grants. This publication, running some 70,000 pages each year, seems more appropriate for someone tracking the progress of a particular grant than for those making their first dive into the polluted waters of federal funding.

• *The Commerce Business Daily*—also printed daily, covers everything of interest to the federal government in terms of contracts. This is something of a twist on the more conventional approach of grant support. Here nonprofit groups may elect to contract with the government to provide services for a wide range of projects on a competitive basis with other organizations, sometimes including private sector corporations.

• *The Federal Assistance Program Retrieval System (FAPRS)*—operated by the Office of Management and Budget, this computer index system searches the *Catalog of Federal Domestic Assistance* for programs of particular interest to your organization. The index is broken into eighty-three subcategories of program specificity, although there are significant gaps, including the arts and aging.

3. *Follow the instructions to the letter.* Most government agencies use complicated application forms which demand scrupulous attention and dedication to detail. Unfortunately, the tortured bureaucratese that passes for instructions will often leave you guessing what they're actually trying to say. Don't guess. If you're uncertain about the instructions, call the office for clarification. (Incidentally, you can also ask to see samples of successful applications from past granting cycles to make certain you're on the right track. However, don't expect this to be easy. Once again, persevere.) Remember: Any error on your application can mean instant disqualification—an easy way for the overworked staff to eliminate many proposals before they're even reviewed.

4. *Calculate the costs of receiving the grant.* Government grants can prove as much a burden as a boon. If you're successful, be prepared for a great deal of paperwork, reporting, and record keeping. And remember that these costs may not be covered in your grant. In fact, they may land your organization in a worse position than you were struggling with prior to receiving the grant.

For example, an arts production agency serving the elderly, institutionalized, and school children recently told us about their trials with a $100,000 grant from their mayor's Office of Economic Development. The grant was awarded after a brilliant lobbying effort. Naturally, the group was ecstatic. However, not a dime of the money could be used for administrative overhead; it could only be spent on artists' stipends. Processing the $100,000 payroll, coordinating several hundred performers for hundreds of separate performances, scheduling, documenting activities, and making extensive reports all took a significant toll on the organization's financial resources. As an additional twist of the knife, the money was awarded on a reimbursement basis. It had to be spent up front, causing a cash flow crisis which the organization could only abate through a bank loan. Unfortunately, this story is by no means unusual.

Foundations

An individual, family, or corporation can shelter and control the use of its excess taxable income, as long as there is agreement to spend the money for broadly defined charitable purposes. To do so, it sets up a private foundation.

But tax advantages are not the only reason why prosperous individuals form foundations. Nonprofit organizations must also reckon with the donor's genuine interest in specific causes or organizations, often to the exclusion of any new project, regardless of its worth. Some individuals unabashedly use their foundations to accrue reputation; they wish to be known by their good works. Others simply want to dispatch the entire matter with as little bother as possible by relegating the review process and check signing to the family attorney.

Today there are about 27,000 active foundations in the United States. They come in all shapes and sizes, but in total they contribute less than 10 percent of the nation's philanthropic dollars. When someone mentions foundations, we're likely to think first of the giants—Ford and Rockefeller and other influential institutions that not only review proposals, but affect public policy throughout the world. And in fact, more than half the funds dispersed annually are granted by less than 2 percent of the nation's foundations. Conversely, over 35 percent of the foundations give away less than 1 percent of the total grant dollars.

In addition to the giants, you'll discover the mid-sized "special interest" institutions such as the Henry J. Kaiser

Foundation, which funds "health-related" projects, or, more eccentrically, the Jockey Club Foundation, which tends to "needy individuals connected with the turf and racing." There are even a few foundations such as the Haymarket Fund in Chicago, Liberty Bell Foundation in Boston, and Vanguard Foundation in San Francisco, which seek out social change projects that may directly challenge the interests of traditional foundation and corporate funders.

However, the big foundations and their special interest counterparts don't often enter the lives of small and mid-sized nonprofit organizations. The Foundation Center (about which, more later) reports that there are 23,455 foundations with assets under $1 million. These relatively small, and slightly larger, foundations are the ones most likely to fund local arts, activist, and social welfare organizations. Small foundations disperse about 70 percent of the grants made annually. Most of these grants are under $1,000, and many are routinely given to traditional charities such as the Heart Fund or the donor's church or alma mater.

The vast majority of American foundations, and the best bet for fund-seeking nonprofits, are the family foundations of all sizes, nestled in almost every large community throughout the nation. Here it's useful to remember that, although the relatives are usually removed from the daily operations of their foundations, the grant money still flows directly from the coffers of a single family. These foundation grants represent someone's hard-earned money, even if that particular someone is many generations dead.

"We still think of the grants we make as presents from the family," said a staff member of a prominent West Coast family foundation, awarding over a million dollars annually. On the other hand, another foundation officer describes his family's grants as "research and development funds for society." Foundations are as diverse as the families who start them, and each has its own priorities, however obscure they may seem to the general public.

In addition to family foundations, we have in the past ten

years seen the rise of community foundations. Community foundations consist of a number of bequests that are collectively managed for the public good in a limited geographic area, usually a city or county. They enjoy special tax advantages in return for greater accountability, and this mutual benefit to both donors and their communities is one reason why the concept is spreading rapidly. There are now about 250 community foundations operating in the United States, or one for nearly every large metropolitan area. It has been estimated that in the next decade community foundations will control a quarter of the nation's foundation assets. But community foundations are not without problems. Oftentimes the donor attaches many strings to his gift. (The most famous recent case must be that of the California Buck Fund, which provides for several million dollars to be distributed annually for charitable purposes in Marin County, one of the richest counties in the United States.) However, any money not tied up in this manner tends to be directed by community foundations toward a broad range of purposes, usually under the direction of a paid staff.

In sum, foundations still provide great opportunities for nonprofit organizations, particularly in the funding of pilot projects. A final caveat is in order. Although it has been said again and again, it still bears repeating: Foundations (and corporate givers) cannot and will not fill the craters excavated in the social landscape by government cutbacks. Nor have they been quick to reorient their priorities toward the most badly damaged programs. If there is a silver lining, it can be found, ironically, in the stock market. Since the growth of most foundations' principal is tied, at least in part, to the performance of stocks, any improvement in the market means that many foundations find themselves in very healthy shape and looking for attractive projects.

Foundation Roulette: How to Come Up with a Winner

Foundation grants are a gamble. And as with any gamble, the odds are with the house, never the player. However, there are a number of steps that can be taken to whittle away the risk. Nobody should play the foundation game without some assurance of at least the *possibility* of an adequate payoff.

1. Decide frankly whether it's worth the trouble. The process of applying for a grant should only be undertaken within the context of an organizational plan. (See Chapter 4, Long-Range Planning.) Any grant worth writing will probably dislocate some organizational resources. It will make demands upon staff, and it will take money to spend the money. (Don't forget bookkeeping, administration, and the like.)

But assuming you've got your plan in place, there are two questions which must now be answered: (1) Does the project for which we're applying fit logically and coherently into the organizational mission? and (2) Have we considered all other means of financially supporting the project? If you can answer both questions affirmatively with a clear conscience, then it's time to move on to the next step.

2. Do enough—but not too much—research. In North America we are blessed with four central offices (located in New York, Washington, Cleveland, and San Francisco) and ninety regional collections of the Foundation Center. The Foundation Center libraries house virtually all the research available on foundation fundraising. Contact their central office for the library nearest you in the United States, Canada, Puerto Rico, and the Virgin Islands (the Foundation Center, 888 Seventh Avenue, New York, New York 10019, 212-975-1120). In addition, many public libraries and universities stock limited materials that can aid foundation research. Install yourself in a well-lit corner and start thumbing through the following guides:

• *The Foundation Directory.* This fat volume contains sketchy information on approximately 2,800 of the largest U.S. foundations. You'll find the foundation name, address, phone number, assets, amount and range of grants, trustees, and some detail about application procedures. The directory is extensively indexed by foundation, location, and grant type.

• *Foundation Center Source Book Profiles.* These monthly analyses of the larger foundations provide more extensive information regarding funding interests, procedures, and histories.

• *The Foundation Center National Data Books (2 volumes).* These provide the most complete listing of foundations throughout the nation, containing more than 22,000 entries. However, the information provided is exceedingly brief. The data books (arranged alphabetically in volume 1, and by state and size in volume 2) are most useful for simply locating funders within your geographic area.

• *The Foundation Grants Index.* This annual guide covers grants of $5,000 or more made by approximately four hundred foundations reporting to the Foundation Center. Estimates claim that the index covers 35 percent of all foundation grants awarded during the year and 65 percent of all grants $5,000 and over. Grant awards are also listed in the bimonthly magazine, *Foundation News.* A cross-index of foundation names, states, recipients, and key words enables the researcher to locate grants of relevance to his field.

• *Comsearch Printouts.* The Foundation Center also breaks down the information provided in the *Grants Index* in computer printouts divided into nine subject areas (Education, Health, Humanities, and others) and subdivided into over a hundred more categories for rapid referral. (For instance, under Welfare, you can locate grants specially given to projects involving "crime and delinquency," "animal welfare," "recreation, camps, and athletics," and others.)

• *Regional Grants Guide.* Some states with a large number of foundations (and an active and responsible funding community) publish guides to foundations within a specific locale. These guides are extremely useful, enabling you to pass over thousands of irrelevant entries contained in the larger guides in favor of the local foundations most likely to review your proposal.

3. *Know your foundation*. Once you've located a potential funder, it's time to dig deeper. You must size up the foundation in terms of the likelihood of its funding *your* organization. You'll need to determine whether the foundation is interested in the population that you serve. Does the topic of your proposal fit the foundation's past giving record? Will it donate for capital improvements? (Few do.) Or general operating expenses? (Fewer still.) How about research funds, or seed money? Does the foundation make grants in the required monetary range? (If their largest grant last year was $200, you're wasting your time with a $5,000 request.) What are its funding deadlines? (If you miss the foundation's funding cycle, your proposal will be shunted away for later review, or in the case of government grants, disqualified. Even worse, your organization loses credibility for the next time around.) Perhaps most importantly, does the foundation fund in your geographic area?

Annual reports issued by the foundations themselves are invaluable; but only 3 percent bother to publish one. The annual Form 990s filed with the IRS can also provide useful analysis of how a foundation actually operates—whom it funds over the year and for how much. (You can also locate the 990s at the Foundation Center.)

The essential question that you seek to answer is this: Does the foundation actually behave in a manner consistent with its claims? Foundations, like all of us, may call themselves one thing, yet act in quite another manner. (It's hardly unusual to find a small family foundation that reports an interest in broad charitable activities, yet gives all of its money every year to the same favored institution.) A major portion of your research involves determining whether your prospective funder's stated goals jibe with its record of donations.

It should be noted that most grant-seekers pay too little attention to this research. Indeed, foundations report that nearly 80 percent of their appeals receive "letters of declension": form letters stating that the proposal "does not fit our needs at this time" or some other equally disappointing stock disclaimer.

4. *Use the staff to your advantage.* The presence of a paid staff will almost always work to your advantage, if you've written a good proposal. Unfortunately, only 5 percent of all foundations employ a staff person. In these happy instances, your life will be made easier by being able to phone the foundation to ask questions. You might even emerge as a known quantity, a person rather than another manila folder taking up valuable space on an already-cluttered desk. In fact, a paid staff—even one person with a part-time secretary—indicates that the foundation is interested in creative uses for its money, and will give proposals the thorough review that they deserve.

5. *Appeal to the self-interest of the funder.* Foundations are obliged to give away their money. And most foundations want their gifts to make a difference, to be money well spent. This means that your proposal should present a unique opportunity for the *foundation.* Of course, it will help your organization and the people whom you serve, and perhaps, by extension, all humanity. But don't forget the appeal to that powerful, ubiquitous human instinct: self-interest. Everyone likes to back a winner.

This does not mean that you should claim any sort of entitlement to the money. No approach could be worse. It does mean that your relationship with the foundation should be based upon reciprocity. There should be benefits and obligations for both parties.

WRITING THE PROPOSAL

As we've tried to stress, there's no voodoo to grant writing. Clear thinking, clean prose, sincerity, and the ability to complete the proposed project are the essential elements of good grantsmanship. Some funders—notably the government and a few large foundations—provide specific guidelines for proposals. Others rely upon a standard format that we'll encounter in a moment. For now, let's review several of the questions most commonly raised about proposal writing.

Who Should Write the Proposal?

If you don't have a development director, either on staff or working as a volunteer, then the proposal should be a collaborative effort which might include staff, Board, and possibly even community members affected by the project. The proposal should first be roughed out by the people with the information about program content, budget, supporting statistics, and evidence of need. But don't *write* the proposal by committee. The actual construction of the working draft should be left to a single person—a good writer, fully apprised of the implications of the project. In general, unless the project is very technical, you won't need to hire a professional proposal writer. One of the strengths of your proposal will be speaking with the authentic voice of your organization. Readers should be able to feel your enthusiasm, energy, and commitment. And this is best accomplished by someone inside your organization.

What Kinds of Proposals Work Best?

Some proposals are written to cover internal needs, such as the cost of computerizing a billing system, or hiring a bookkeeper, or extending capital improvements on a building or equipment. Others—in fact, the vast majority of successful proposals—address external needs. By this we mean projects which serve your constituency, right a wrong, contribute to the commonweal. In general, it's easier to receive first-time funding for a project directed toward external needs. Once you've developed a relationship with the foundation, it's more likely that they'll prove sympathetic to your internal needs. The foundation will begin to care about your existence, even your survival.

How Do We Make Contact?

The letter of inquiry—the most conventional means of making the initial contact with a foundation—is the subject of some controversy. Some fundraisers feel it should be used in all cases. Others believe that it only gives the funder an opportunity to turn you down before the full proposal has reached their hands. Use this as a good first rule: If the foundation has a staff, send a letter of inquiry; if there is no staff, you'll probably do better to give them the full proposal.

The letter of inquiry *must* be addressed to a specific person. ("Dear Friend," "Sir, Madam, or Ms.," or "To Whom It May Concern" are always inappropriate.) Following the greeting, the reader should encounter one or two pages of vivid, cogent writing that fully describes your organization, its mission, and the project that you intend to propose to the foundation. Also include the cost of the project, and the reasons why you believe that this particular foundation might be interested in reading the full proposal. (Let them see that you've done your homework.) Enclose your organization's brochure and perhaps one other piece of information, such as a list of your Board of Directors (if it's impressive and broadly representative of your community), or a recent newspaper feature article covering your work, or some outside source giving credibility to the problem you plan to address.

The letter closes with your name, an indication of your willingness to meet and discuss the project, and a promise to call within two weeks. This call is to establish your seriousness and personalize the application. Ask if the letter was received, if you can provide further information, and when you can expect to hear from the foundation. If you are given the opportunity, expand on the letter; but if not, don't push it.

What Does the Funder Look For?

First and foremost, the foundation officer will determine how well your proposal fits the foundation's guidelines and priorities. Then she'll look at the competence, integrity, and track record of the organization. She's trying to answer the all-important question: Can this group really pull it off? Next, the impact of the project itself will be considered. Who will benefit? Given all the other pressing needs in the community, is this project really worth funding? Is it creatively conceived, cost-effective, perhaps a model for other communities?

Finally, the foundation reviewer will look for *energy*—the commitment and dynamism of the people who will carry out the work. Even when foundations have relatively clear criteria for review, their subjective judgments will always come into play. Thus, the more alive your proposal feels to the reader, the better your chances of drawing attention, interest, and ultimate support.

In short, the combination of credibility, competence, and inspiration should be woven through every aspect of the proposal.

Is There Anything I Shouldn't Say?

Yes! Never say:

• "If you don't give us money, we'll go under." Foundations are understandably reluctant to plug the respirators into a moribund organization.

• "Here's a list of what we need. What can you help us with?" The most successful proposals are tailored to the funder's guidelines. (That's why you did all that research, remember?)

• "Will you look at a draft of our proposal and tell us if you can fund it, or how we can change it?" Funders will gladly read your proposal, but they won't write it for you. Nor will they be interested in hearing their own words parroted back at them after providing a critique of your incoherent first draft.

Can We Get a Personal Interview with the Foundation?

Maybe. But it will require much polite, tenacious effort offset by a willingness to take no for an answer. If you do succeed in setting up a meeting, it will usually prove a great advantage and a good omen for the future. Take along your most knowledgeable and charming Board member. Prepare by imagining the hardest, most embarrassing, and even dumbest questions you could be asked. Your answers should be clear, brief, and honest. After all, your group *wants* to tackle this project. There's no excuse for being anything less than totally prepared.

You'll also want to listen very closely to what the funder is saying. By way of illustration we recall the cautionary tale of a struggling community arts journal. Lucky enough to get an interview with the director of a small family foundation, they went in with all flags flying, and reams of financial information to support their contention that, with a little boost from the foundation, they could soon be self-supporting from subscriptions and ad revenues. Three-year revenue predictions were unveiled, as were cash flow statements developed with painstaking precision.

"I was interested in the financial stability, of course," the funder said later, "but what excited me about the journal was its potential to do significant art criticism and even investigative journalism. I thought I was being clear, but every time I asked about their content, I got a speech about revenue development, or their computerized mailing list." A sad tale of failed grantsmanship.

Strive to establish a dialogue, allowing room for creative alternatives, such as matching money or technical assistance. At some point in the meeting, the funder may suggest that although she's not interested in your current proposal, there's another related project that she thinks might be fundable. Resist the urge to jump at the money. Thank her for her suggestion; and tell her you find it very interesting and that you'll get back to her. It's always a bad idea to strike a deal on the spur of the moment for something you haven't thoroughly considered.

Figure a half-hour for your meeting and don't overstay your welcome. After all, your chief aim is to put faces and personalities behind the words of your application. Exude professionalism, warmth, and optimism. In short, be the kind of person to whom *you'd* want to give money. And finally, if the grant is not forthcoming, ask, ever-politely, why. Explore the possibility of reapplying. You can also ask if there are other sources known to the funder that might be interested in your project. Keep the lines of communication open. Eventually, it'll pay off.

What Should We Do to Follow Up?

Write a formal thank-you letter to the foundation's director and personal letters to any staff members with whom you had contact. It seems astounding, but nevertheless many organizations fail to comply with this basic courtesy. Check with the foundation about how they wish to be credited on your published materials. If they want recognition, be absolutely scrupulous about including the foundation's name in appropriate press releases, newsletters, brochures, and other materials that will hit the public eye. Add the foundation to your mailing list to make certain that they'll actually see these acknowledgments.

Conform to the reporting requirements of the foundation. If you must change significant aspects of your proposed project, consult the foundation. Don't assume that they won't find out. (They will.) And anyway, the chances are that they'll approve alternate plans if you clearly explain the reasons behind the change. Of course, a final report at the end of the grant period should conclude the project. Make it as brief as possible, while being complete. Include any negative findings as well as positive results, and follow your evaluation plan as closely as possible.

Most of all, do your very best to make certain that your project is a success. Not merely a success on paper, for the benefit of the funder, but an actual contribution to the community. After all, that's why you're in business. The relationship with your foundation is one you'll continue to nurture through regular communication and complete honesty. And although few foundations wish to fund any group in perpetuity, a funder who trusts you and your work will have a stake in your organization's future. This person—and institution—should be treated as a strong and trusted ally.

As one major national funder told us recently, "Most agencies think of a proposal as a one-shot deal, and that's a mistake. Good grant-making is about long-term relationships."

Format

There are any number of ways to construct a useful grant proposal. And while government agencies generally provide very specific funding guidelines, foundations now respond to the full complement of grant-writing styles, providing that they inform, interest, and inspire the reader.

The body of the proposal should not be photocopied, although supporting documents may be. Do not include expensive graphics or bulky printed documents unless they are directly pertinent to your credibility or the project's design. Fancy portfolios are unnecessary, and it's a bad idea to put the proposal in a permanent binding—it will only have to be taken apart to be photocopied by the foundation staff.

Bearing all this in mind, we now offer our standard format for the beginning proposal writer. This particular model breaks the proposal into ten major sections. You may wish to combine some of these elements, add others, eliminate some altogether. Play with the model; it's only one of several that are commonly used today. Adapt it to your organization's needs. Let it work for you.

1. Cover Letter

This might be similar to the letter of inquiry, a brief introduction to your organization and the proposed project, whetting the appetite for more details. The letter should also include the name and phone number of a contact person within your organization. Needless to say—but we'll say it anyway—this individual should be intimate with the details of the proposal.

2. Organizational History

Employ here brevity, candor, and enthusiasm regarding the mission, structure, and accomplishments of your organization.

Presume that the funder knows nothing about your work, regardless of your sterling reputation. Provide hard data—numbers served, constituency composition, annual operating budget—as well as anecdotal and descriptive information.

3. Project Description

This is the key section of the proposal. Here you include a compact, compelling narrative covering the project's goals and objectives and the specific activities you'll undertake to achieve them. The tone of this section should be warmly professional, caring but not cloying. In general, the judicious use of specific examples (number of users, times, dates, hours of client contact, etc.) will make the case much better than elaborate generalities.

Although this task might sound formidable, the facts of the proposal should be very easy to write. The important information will have been thoroughly considered during your initial planning; the details will have survived Board scrutiny and the broad range of questions that they'll have asked, including:

- Why is this project needed?
- Is our organization the right group to attempt it?
- What will the the short-and long-term costs?
- What are the available income sources for the project?
- Is anyone else doing the same thing?
- What are the benefits for our constituents? For our organization?
- How will we ensure the quality of the service that we propose to provide? How will we evaluate our effectiveness?
- If the program succeeds, how will the community be changed? What are the larger implications of success or failure?

Of course, the answers to these questions should be backed up with as many facts, figures, and testimonials as you need to make your case. But not more than you need. Otherwise, the proposal becomes top-heavy with data and the human benefits are lost in a fog of numbers.

4. Budget

As we've said before, the budget is the numerical translation of your planning. It should be accurate and specific. If there are budget categories which seem unusually high or low, explain them. Do not include large amounts under a "miscellaneous" category. Foundation people look at hundreds of budgets each year; they can spot the soft spots immediately. (See the budget preparation section in Chapter 3.)

Fudging the numbers will erode the credibility of the most intriguing narrative. Stick as close as possible to genuine market value estimates. And offer no surprises; all budget items should be referred to in (or at least logically inferable from) the project description. In addition, you must be certain that the budget makes sense within the context of your entire organization. No funder will be likely to give you more than 10–20 percent of your annual budget for any one project, and it will probably contribute considerably less.

Finally, give some thought to future funding. Attach a statement describing how the project might be funded after the requested grant support ends. This might include plans for developing new income sources, special fundraising, or fees for service. If you can, suggest ways in which the grant might leverage other funds for the project; or how the program could eventually become self-sufficient. Since most foundations are not interested in long-term funding—and indeed, may turn down an otherwise promising application if they fear they'll be stuck with it for the duration—it pays to invest considerable thought in this matter.

5. Resumes of Key Staff Involved with Project

Evidence of the capability and experience of your people will build confidence in the project.

6. Evaluation Plan

This section complements the project narrative. It need not be an elaborate statistical exercise. You simply want to tell the funder how you'll know if the project is successful. What will you measure, how will the measurement be conducted, and who will be responsible for its implementation? Obviously some projects are more conducive to quantitative analysis than others. But even if you're looking for intangibles such as attitudinal change, you must demonstrate some means of determining whether you've accomplished what you set out to do.

7. Board Authorization

Attach a letter signed by the president of your Board of Directors authorizing the proposal's submission. Include a list of your Board members and their affiliations in the community as well as a short statement describing the Board's involvement with the project and their ultimate responsibility for its success. Once again, you are acting to bolster the confidence of the funder.

8. Financial Statements

Some funders require an audited statement. This is certainly preferable if your annual budget reaches above $100,000. However, an unaudited statement will serve many other funders as long as your information is complete and clearly presented. In any case, include a breakdown of earned and contributed income and, if possible, a summary of the past three years' financial activity. Every potential funder wants to know exactly where your money comes from and who has already supported you.

9. Tax-Exempt Status

Attach a copy of your organization's IRS 501(c)3 tax exemption letter. If you are using another tax-exempt nonprofit organization as a fiscal agent for your activities, use its letter and a single page agreement stating the terms of your relationship.

10. Supporting Materials

These items should give your organization color and depth in the imagination of the reader. You might include:
• A brochure or annual report

• Copies of newspaper and magazine articles about your group's work

• Your very best letters of support from selected constituents (Caution: These letters should be genuine contributions from people knowledgeable about your work. A slew of "formula" letters or testimonials from politicians or local figureheads can be detrimental.)

• One to three great photographs, if your organization or project lends itself to visual representation. However, do not use pictures if they're less than smashing.

A final word about proposal writing: The secret to a great proposal is not the caliber of the prose, or the amount of documentation, or even the magnitude of the project's need. It is the quality of the thinking and planning that goes into the design of the project. The great proposal emanates from the heart of the organization. After days, weeks, and perhaps even months of meticulous planning, the appropriate proposal almost seems to write itself.

ADDITIONAL RESOURCES

"Program Planning and Proposal Writing" by Norton J. Kiritz. 1980. The Grantsmanship Center, 1031 South Grand Avenue, Los Angeles, CA 90015.

Among the dozens of useful books and artiicles about proposal writing that we've seen, this reprint from *The Grantsmanship Center News* is the very best. It's concise (under fifty pages), jargon-free, and extremely well organized. For the moment, you can do no better than to read Norton Kiritz's guide. And when something better does come along, the odds are good that Kiritz will have a hand in that too.

Foundation Fundamentals: A Guide for Grantseekers by Carol M. Kurzig. 1980. The Foundation Center, 888 Seventh Avenue, New York, NY 10106.

The bible for foundation research, written by the people who should know.

8

* *

SURVIVAL TACTICS

Self-sufficiency in an age of scarcity

**Crisis is equally composed of danger and
opportunity.** —*Chinese proverb*

After twenty years of healthy growth and rapid progress, many
nonprofit organizations jauntily turned the corner into the
1980s and came face to face with questions of survival.

First, the federal government began its withdrawal. The
CETA public service employment program ground to an
abrupt halt. Applications for "emergency aid" clogged foundation mail rooms across the country. Soon organizations in
every area of health, human services, education, and the arts
found themselves thrown together in a funding free-for-all,
with the winners taking home ever-thinner slices of the incredible shrinking pie.

More than $33 billion in government funding, according
to the Urban Institute, will be lost to the nonprofit sector
throughout the mid-1980s. And while this reduction con-
stitutes only a 5 percent cut for the nonprofit sector as a
whole, it represents a loss of more than 50 percent for social
service and community development projects. In other words,
the brunt of federal economies has been borne by those who
most need funding assistance, and whose ability to generate
new income is severely limited.

Since the decade began, many analysts have advanced the notion that nonprofits must share the blame for their new fiscal misery. Criticisms formerly leveled at government are now directed toward the needy nonprofit sector. Nonprofit organizations, it is charged, fail to carry their own weight. They are backwards and sometimes inefficient. They substitute a softhearted and, by implication, softheaded liberalism for the toughness required to survive in the "real world" of the marketplace. A classic case of blaming the victim prevails.

At the same time, economic theorists ranging from Milton Friedman to socialist Michael Harrington discount not only the ability of corporate largess to fill the gap left by the federal government, but the wisdom of asking it to. On the Left grow fears of further cooption. The Right remains confident that competition will adjust market demand, enabling the most productive groups to stay afloat while pushing others to the bottom.

The Darwinian message is clear: Nonprofits must become more self-sufficient, and they better do it fast. In its undiluted form, the medicine seems hard to swallow. "Self-sufficient?" ask nonprofit organizers everywhere. "But don't we do work that benefits people who can't possibly pay market value for our services? After all, we're not General Motors."

Bitter as this pill seems, its side effects include some important insights. Smart organizers have begun thinking about the income-generating tools they'll use to survive the decade.

WHAT IS SELF-SUFFICIENCY?

In a world increasingly dominated by multinational corporations and complex unions of public and private enterprise, it sounds almost romantic and a little naive to talk about the "self-sufficient organization." What we're really addressing is the need to raise earned income levels, or money received in exchange for our goods and services.

No wonder nonprofit managers shudder at the prospect. Suddenly it's not enough to work endless hours at ridiculous salaries for the public good. Now we must also become market analysts, retailers, and salespeople. Isn't this the fate we entered the nonprofit sector to avoid?

In fact, nonprofits already earn a great deal of their income. According to the Brookings Institution, nonprofits raked in more than $90 billion in 1980 through fees, interest, investments, and other sources. Of course, the larger institutions, such as universities and hospitals, account for the lion's share in real dollars. But many small organizations also boast earned income levels on a par with the national average.

The demands of the marketplace may seem formidable to the novice entrepreneur. But if we break down the elements of self-sufficiency planning into manageable bites, we can see that several of the major strategies closely relate to our present skills. Today, nonprofit groups are increasing their earned income by:

- Marketing established services
- Starting up profit-making sidelines
- Constructing new business ventures

Perhaps only a small percentage of the nation's nonprofits enjoy the resources and opportunities to earn the majority of their annual budget. Even for them, as we shall see, there are no surefire schemes. But in sum, these profit-enhancing efforts, combined with an effective fundraising program, may produce the strongest approximation to self-reliance possible in our complicated, interdependent world.

MARKETING THE NONPROFIT SECTOR

"Nonprofit organizations," says Ben Shute of the Rockefeller Brothers Fund, "should look to the corporate sector for ideas, though not necessarily for models." Nowhere is this distinction more important than in the area of marketing, an activity which usually separates nonprofit sheep from commercial goats in terms of self-image, motivation, and ethics.

The art of promoting what nobody needs has swept innumerable rascals into public office, while supermarket shelves—indeed our very lives—are cluttered with products whose value is negligible, if not actually harmful. And it's largely the result of aggressive marketing. No wonder many of us react negatively to the concept.

But condemning marketing for its results is like blaming a hammer for driving a nail into the wrong plank of wood. Our quarrel is with the carpenter. Upon closer examination, marketing turns out to be an effective means of analyzing the real value of goods and services that nonprofit organizations presume to offer the world. It's also a method of effective promotion. In fact, the most promising future for most nonprofits may lie not so much in fabricating flashy new products, but in the effective presentation of our current strengths and services.

Understanding the Marketing Tool

Oddly enough, many nonprofits that believe themselves receptive to the marketing concept do not understand its full implications. First, marketing is not selling. Marketing places emphasis upon the needs and desires of the consumer.

When a day-care center strives to reach more clients by publishing an attractive brochure to be distributed throughout the public schools, it is engaged in *selling*. It is primarily concerned with promoting its existing services.

Should the same day-care center undertake a survey of parents within its locale; determine that day-care needs vary according to neighborhood, transportation availability, child's age, and parental income; construct a program and several different publicity pieces that speak to these various needs; and *then* begin to persuade new clients to avail themselves of the service; the center has adopted a *marketing strategy*.

Moreover, marketing can assist nonprofit groups in extricating themselves from the familiar circle of self-justification: "If nobody is using our day-care center," runs the impeccable illogic, "it's only because they don't yet understand how helpful we can be."

Solipsisms of this sort blind organizations to the more potent issues of cost, location, scope, vision, and genuine need. Organizations must naturally attend to their own goals, strengths, and weaknesses. But never at the cost of their usefulness to the public. For many groups, the departure from institutional concerns in favor of their clients' articulated needs marks a radical shift that can set about transforming the organization for the good of all.

Creating the Marketing Plan

The first step in constructing a marketing plan is to admit that your product, service, activity, or cause holds no intrinsic value. This may sound like heresy, but it's also the cornerstone of marketing strategy. Only the usefulness of your work—and, even more, its utilization—justify your existence.

Think of it this way: All your lobbying, funding, and program plotting to bring hot meals to seniors comes to naught unless the seniors themselves actually perceive the need and prove willing and able to use the program. All too often, organizations blame their potential "customers" for being too ignorant to avail themselves of critical health services, too uncultured to attend the theater, too apathetic to join political campaigns. But nobody buys to satisfy the seller; we attend to our own needs first. At its best, a marketing approach trusts the consumers/clients/audience to know: what they need, why they need it, how it should be delivered, and whether its quality is acceptable. Like effective community organizing, marketing should be built upon this first principle of self-interest.

Remember, we're not talking about publicity and advertising here. Do not presume that your organization's services remain unused merely because of inadequate publicity. "I always got the blame for small houses," complained the publicist for an East Coast community theater. "The fact was, the reviews were often terrible. And nobody wants to see a lousy show no matter how often they hear about it."

The marketing plan should eliminate this kind of problem. Its primary tools involve client research data, keeping an ear to the community. You can use written questionnaires, phone queries, and personal interviews to:

- Gather demographic information
- Determine why your services are used or ignored by target groups
- Discover what potential clients believe your organization to represent
- Turn up unmet needs related to your purpose

The thrust of inquiry must not be "How can we get you to buy from us?" but rather, "What are your needs within our area of service?" An extensive marketing plan, particularly one which might redirect your group's priorities, can benefit from the use of outside professionals. In this case, familiarity with marketing principles is more important than familiarity with your cause. It will then be up to you to decide if the recommended changes are appropriate to your organization.

Of course, for many of us, the marketing of nonprofit services will not prove sufficient to meet expanding demands for cash and liquidity. At this point, some of our bolder colleagues will take an even more daring step into the brave new world of commerce.

THE ROLE OF NONPROFIT ENTERPRISE

The good news is that there are ways to add profit-making ventures to your annual budget without turning the front office into a boutique or your recreation center into a disco. In most cases, the drive into the marketplace will not signal a revolution in purpose and style. Limited nonprofit enterprise generally doesn't require separate incorporation, new staffing and management, or a substantial outlay of capital.

The key word here is "limited."

Nonprofits enjoy tax benefits and other legal exemptions by operating within the realm of the "public good." And while the nonprofit organizational model might in many ways resemble commercial enterprise, there remains a critical difference in terms of financial support. Nonprofit investors, more commonly known as donors, enjoy a wealth of gratitude, public recognition, good feelings, and even a tax write-off; but they never pocket a dollar in return. In other words, a nonprofit organization, though historically run as a deficit-financed operation, may spin along for years with income well above expenses and not jeopardize its tax-exempt status, providing it follows the gospel according to the IRS.

Your Best Bet: Profit-making Sidelines

In recent years, many large nonprofits, and even small and mid-sized organizations, have attempted business ventures whose financial success feeds the tax-exempt operation. These efforts oftentimes operate as a sideline to the organization's major program concerns. In other instances, they require massive reorganization and extensive capital investment. In every case, the successful nonprofit business begins with a good idea.

Where do these ideas come from?

The nonprofit entrepreneur first wisely consults the obvious: his present resources. If you're serious about starting a business, you'll begin by scrutinizing every aspect and asset of your organization that might further render income through a creative new twist:

Your space. Think of the rental possibilities: offices, meeting rooms, theater, recreation facilities, grounds, etc. Are there off-hour or off-season uses which wouldn't interfere with your nonprofit mission?

Your equipment. Lighting and sound equipment, sports and playground materials, musical instruments, cribs and playpens, or even office machines may prove valuable as short-term rentals. Are there hidden sources of income lurking in your inventory? Don't overlook your nonmaterial resources—photos, logos, copyrights.

Your staff. Of course the people in your organization are already overworked and overwhelmed! But we're not suggesting they start moonlighting as cab drivers or take on a morning paper route. We're talking about using present staff expertise as an income resource. For example: An organization concerned with bettering the conditions of working women has established itself as a leading researcher in the field of office automation, technology, and white-collar health hazards. This group has established a successful consulting program that makes its expertise available, for a fee, to governmental bodies and corporations.

Your relations with the public. If your organization has any foot traffic—parents dropping their children off for day-care, clients showing up for their clinic appointments, audiences for a show—consider the market for secondary services. It's long been an axiom in the commercial theater and sports that the real money is in concessions. They can be anything from food and drink to buttons, T-shirts, publications, handcrafts, or convenience store items.

Your clients and volunteers. Organizations such as psychiatric halfway houses or substance abuse centers have founded restaurants, hauling services, and retail outfits staffed by the nonprofit's clients as a component of their treatment program. A number of groups operate thrift shops, stocked entirely through donations, and staffed completely by volunteers.

The field appears wide open, with income opportunities bounded only by imagination and hard work. But running a business sideline has some hidden difficulties. First, there are tax implications. The IRS tolerates nonprofit enterprise providing that business activities "contribute importantly" to the organization's chartered, tax-exempt goals. Most of the examples given above could fall into this category, as might related businesses, such as an environmental group's sale of calendars promoting conservationist themes, or a day-care center's line of handcrafted, safety-tested toys.

Some organizations skirt the issue entirely by opening unrelated businesses under the auspices of a separate, for-profit corporation. Of course, this enterprise is liable for income tax, while enjoying none of the advantages open to an exempt organization. In any case, remember this: Interpretation of tax laws demands professional legal assistance. No organization should bumble into the marketplace without a clear delineation of the potential hazards, lest they find themselves in the position of the Southwestern Native American organization that for years successfully financed its scholarship program with oil lease trading until its tax-exempt status was revoked.

Starting Your Own Business

And now the bad news: No less an authority than the U.S. government's Small Business Administration informs us that nine out of ten new businesses fail. Pause for a moment to ponder this statistic before you leap into T-shirt and postcard production. Look around for the 450,000 businesses that opened in 1981. Only 45,000 are still functioning.

These statistics may be daunting, but they do not indicate the full measure of peril. SBA estimates cover the entire range of small business efforts. Enterprises initiated by nonprofits—short on capital, experience, and perhaps the brand of cutthroat ambition needed to turn a profit—face a fate even more dire. "The overwhelming evidence," concludes Charles Cagnon's study, *Business Ventures of Citizen Groups*, "is that most nonprofit groups have failed in their attempts to develop financially viable businesses."

All of this speaks to the very great need for caution. Ill-considered business ventures have ushered dozens of ambitious nonprofits into bankruptcy court. Many hundreds of others now conclude that the small financial reward was simply not worth the effort. However, the strongly motivated organization need not slink away in despair. Most nonprofit business consultants, while arguing over the number of organizations that may succeed in the marketplace, agree that many of the predators that threaten youthful businesses can be identified and avoided with foresight and planning.

Not Enough Money Most organizations enter their new business ventures with enthusiasm, high hopes, and very little financial backing. But sound business practice demands planning for capital needs over several years of operation. Even a successful business may take three to five years to realize a small return of 5 percent or less.

Capital requirements should be differentiated. Unlike the small community service project that tends towards labor-intensive programs, all too often financed from a single pot of co-mingled funds, the serious business venture must plan for a vast array of unpredictable expenses. You'll need to consider the fluctuating demands of cash, equipment, building and land use, and inventory, and provide a sizeable cushion to cover accounts receivable and expansion needs. (Come to think of it, you should have planned for these same needs with your nonprofit group, although, in the beginning, you almost certainly did not.) However, the business world tends to have a more voracious appetite. Undercapitalization, unless eliminated from the very beginning, will stalk your fledgling enterprise like a hungry wolf.

Too Little Time   If you're searching for a quick fix, then stay away from business ventures. Hold a benefit, raffle, or garage sale, but don't open a shop or start a catering service. Successful businesses demand organizational nurturance, time, and patience. Keep in mind that you are building a brand new organization within the old one.

Ask: Can staff really afford to devote two hours daily in order to prop up the business? Is the executive director willing to spend evenings and weekends on matters entirely concerned with the pursuit of profits? Is the Board prepared to give the business the years it may need to prove itself? Don't try to compensate for undercapitalization with unrealistic allotments of donated time. If anything, be prepared to pay adequately for the many chores which your people will not have the leisure to handle.

Inexperienced and Inappropriate Management   The typical career arc of the small nonprofit manager includes several years in the organizational trenches (whether called direct service, program delivery, or educational/artistic staff), followed by a great leap forward, as often as not propelled by organizational crisis. While the sink-or-swim school of management training may produce fine administrators in spite of itself, there is no reason to be optimistic that an inexperienced manager will be able to overcome a lack of business training. "We advise people to first learn how to run their nonprofit organizations before they take on a business venture," cautions Paula Hammett of The Youth Project. Even then, the best management decision may be to farm out the new business to an appropriately experienced individual, possibly someone from the outside who shares the vision of your organization, if not the direct experience of your staff.

Here we encounter another critical question: Are you prepared to pay the management of your business as much as or more than the director and staff of your nonprofit? A survey conducted by the Neighborhood Development Collaborative indicates that most small nonprofits find their profit-making enterprises require changes in management or staff. Some groups even form a separate Board of Directors to oversee the business, placing emphasis upon commercial backgrounds and a narrow spectrum of related skills, as opposed to the broad representation usually sought for the nonprofit Board.

Confusion About the Role of the New Business Disruption accompanies the most felicitous of changes. When change involves an incursion into the teeming and uncharted marketplace, unprecedented confusion may result regarding aims and means. Staff may evince ignorance, even active hostility to the "business world." New people hired for their commercial expertise may find themselves at odds with staff who see themselves as holding down the front lines, fighting the real battle. Board members may even interpret a profitable business venture as a shift in the group's goals. Success, as well as failure, can cut to the soul of an organization.

This tail-wagging-the-dog syndrome can lead to a loss of

energy and direction unless the organizational mission, staff morale, and Board commitment are extremely stable and dependable. We are also obliged to point out that this whole area drives some funders crazy. Certainly your foundation, government, and individual contributors want you to succeed. They want you to develop healthy sources of earned revenue. They want to see you decrease your dependence on them. But psychologically it's hard for even the most enlightened donor to get past the image of a bustling restaurant or mail order business to see the struggling nonprofit behind it.

All of this is not to suggest that developing a business is necessarily a bad idea. But undoubtedly it will prove a *new* idea. And that means that care and planning must prevail.

One more caveat: The careful thought that goes into developing a business must include a plan for presenting the organization's new face to the outside world in a way that does not diminish the image of the nonprofit parent. Obviously those most affected by the new business need to be apprised of the changes and possibly be included in planning. Most important, the new business must not run counter to the organization's philosophy and programs, either in its content or its style of management.

One gross example: Some nonprofit groups have successfully undertaken franchise agreements with McDonald's and other fast food chains. Clearly, this would be a poor venture for a group concerned with nutrition education, or even neighborhood littering. More subtly, however, this sort of venture would be equally inappropriate for any group concerned with labor issues or innovative management techniques, since the franchise model requires rigid adherence to hierarchical structure and assembly line job functions.

"Small isn't beautiful," says Loren Cole, Executive Director of Inquiring Systems, a West Coast consulting firm helping nonprofits to develop self-sufficiency schemes. "Compatible is beautiful."

The Great Exception: When Nonprofit Businesses Succeed

Not surprisingly, nonprofit commercial success reflects the experience of traditional for-profit entrepreneurs. In this respect, we have a good deal to learn from the business world. However, after solving the conventional problems of money, time, management, and purpose, the nonprofit businessperson must examine some additional hard issues:

Commitment   The business of nonprofit organizations will never be business. Nonprofit organizations enjoy their special status in service to the community. When the business sideline, or for that matter the development office, gains sway over the objectives of the organization, then the reasons for continuing need to be reviewed.

Now here comes the real problem. Any small business destined to attain even modest success—and most ventures can expect to see no more than a 5–10 percent return after several years—requires fanatical devotion to all phases of planning and operation. Can one muster the requisite fanaticism to run both a valuable public service program and an efficient business? The answer for most organizations is no, at least not over the necessary months running into years of overtime hours, missed holidays, and postponed vacations, all with no guarantee of reward.

Nonprofit businesspeople, regardless of their dedication, simply do not place themselves in the same kind of personal jeopardy that compels endless hours of extra labor from the commercial entrepreneur. A nonprofit manager, serving at the pleasure of the Board, is understandably unwilling to risk physical health and financial ruin for a thrift shop or a line of T-shirts or a hot dog stand. Even Board members generally avoid suffering individually for the bad debts of the corporation. Fear, one of the great human motivators, never bares its full set of teeth under these conditions.

Many successful nonprofit businesses avoid the issue of

double-time commitment by artfully drawing together organizational purpose and commercial ingenuity. When the National Women's History Project completes another sale through its mail order catalog, it not only enhances the financial resources of the organization, but also advances public awareness of women's contributions in American history. When Rubicon, a mental health service organization, sells yet another potted plant from its garden nursery, it serves both the developmental and rehabilitative goals of its clients-employed-as-staff, as well as contributing to financial stability for the organization.

The perfect dual-purpose enterprise may not prove immediately accessible to your group; it's the rare organization that kills these two birds with a single ingenious stone. However, when commercial and organizational purpose appear worlds apart (as in the case of the small private school that planned to market canned fish from Australia) then you need to take a second look at the resources being drained from your *real* work.

Expectations You start a business to make money. Period. There is no other acceptable reason. While you may accrue benefits in terms of visibility, public relations, important funding contacts, and even community service, these bonuses should never serve as motivating factors in the long, sweaty process of setting up shop. "We lost $2,000 in a series of community concerts," said one improbably optimistic nonprofit entrepreneur, "but the benefits in good publicity were incalculable." Exactly.

Market Sense and Common Sense Before charging into the marketplace, you must determine whether your proposed venture has any real potential. In other words: You may be selling, but is anybody buying? Who are your customers? How many exist in an ideal market? In today's market? Do they have money to spend on your product? Sophisticated market surveys, the kind of research always undertaken by the likes of Proctor and Gamble before entering a new market or introducing a new product, may not be feasible with your limited front money and untrained personnel. (Though perhaps it's time to recruit a marketing executive to your Board. . . .)

You can, however, at least apply common sense and simple calculations to your own crude market appraisal. Can your community support another restaurant? How many restaurants opened and closed during the last three years? Does your proposed location attract the same patrons as your proposed menu? Remember, your goal is not to gather information which will support your contention that a restaurant is a good idea. Rather, you must decide whether to proceed with your initial planning. Does a need exist? Go into the research with as few preconceptions as possible if you want reliable data. Do not allow your own ego involvement, or that of anyone associated with the group, to keep you from getting unbiased information.

Ask questions relentlessly. Excavate data from city records. Collar the proprietors of like endeavors, both successful and faltering, to pinpoint the concerns pertinent to your particular venture. For example, most nonprofit people know nothing about pricing. After all, none of their clients pay what the goods or services really cost. It can be hard to shake this subsidized service attitude, but you'd better learn to do it or face bankruptcy.

For assistance on specific issues, contact local representatives from Service Corps of Retired Executives (SCORE) or Active Corps of Executives (ACE), or other volunteer programs making business acumen and experience accessible to newborn enterprises. Although these groups are not necessarily specialists in nonprofit businesses, with enough questions and good fortune, you may locate an appropriate volunteer expert.

The Small Business Administration also publishes nearly one hundred free booklets on a range of financial and management issues, from inventory to marketing and staffing. They also offer bibliographies for various kinds of businesses, from bookstores to restaurants and handcrafts.

The point here is to admit that you know nothing, and to proceed as if you plan to risk everything—which, in fact, you might. You, or someone in the organization, must become an expert on minutiae that would not have held your attention for thirty seconds six months ago.

And Now . . . the Business Plan

If you're still serious about this—you've done a lot of research, located your market, lined up front capital and Board support, and convinced all your friends to buy one—then it's perhaps time to construct a solid business plan.

Your business plan should include:
- A description of your product or service
- A market analysis
- Management strategy
- Promotional tactics
- Monthly cash flow projections for the first year
- Cost, income, and profit/loss estimates for three to five years
- Reasonable expectations for growth, and plans to meet the organizational and fiscal demands that accompany growth

To do all this you will probably need to take Dear Abby's most common advice: Seek professional help. The business plan you need probably isn't something your business manager can do in his spare time. First, he doesn't have any spare time. Second, he doesn't know how to do it anyway. The money spent in having someone from the outside—perhaps someone from the for-profit sector who does business planning and marketing for a living, or someone specializing in non-profit business—will be small compared to your investment in the business itself. Of course you won't neglect to check your consultant's references, talk to businesses that have used his services, and make sure you're sympatico.

Once your plan is written down, pass it under eyes more

discriminating than your own. Revise the plan. Refine it. Great variance between your dreams and the bottom line reality spelled out by your plan will signal financial disaster. The first duty of the business plan is to tell you not how to run your new enterprise, but whether you should risk the effort at all.

THE LIMITATIONS OF THE MARKETPLACE

The idea of the marketplace has recently stimulated thought and enlivened action in the nonprofit world. For a few groups gifted with ingenuity, pluck, planning expertise, capital, and good fortune, the considerable risks of business will occasionally produce blue-chip profits. Sadly though, many other groups will find great difficulty in earning a return on their market ventures. Some will fail altogether, or be driven deeper into the red.

There are also other, more subtle limitations.

Lest we forget: The marketplace simply does not provide for the entire range of human aspiration, expression, and need. To some extent that is why the nonprofit sector exists.

It would be a fine thing indeed for most nonprofits to be able to earn the greater part of their annual budgets. The payoff would come not only in dollars, but in experience, contacts, and that compelling, if somewhat ill-defined American virtue: self-reliance. But if nonprofits flock to the marketplace, succeed financially, and yet lose their souls, what have we gained? Will the drive to market services mean the abandonment of low-income constituencies in favor of a middle-class clientele better positioned to pay? Might this wholesale celebration of market values further threaten marginal organizations on whom society depends to urge public policy toward more humane goals?

Where was the "market" for civil rights in Mississippi in 1955? How about for American troop withdrawal from Vietnam in 1965? Dow Chemical and Honeywell would never have introduced these "products"! Activists had to create their own markets. And the challenge, then as now, was to organize the community in its own best interests—above its own restrictive self-image, and beyond the conventional wisdom. In addition to financial concerns, nonprofit groups must also adhere to a strict ethical bottom line. We must constantly ask ourselves: Do we still *deserve* to be in business?

ADDITIONAL RESOURCES

Marketing in Nonprofit Organizations edited by Patrick J. Montana. 1979. Amacon (a division of American Management Associations), 135 West 50th Street, New York, NY 10020.

A good introduction to marketing throughout the nonprofit world. Tends to cover efforts of large organizations, but the principles expounded may be adapted for more modest projects.

"Nonprofits: Check Your Attention to Customers" by Alan R. Andreasen. *The Grantsmanship Center News*, Nov./Dec. 1982 (reprinted from *Harvard Business Review*, May/June 1982). The Grantsmanship Center, 1031 South Grand Avenue, Los Angeles, CA 90015.

An interesting analysis of marketing principles applied to nonprofit organizations of various sizes.

Business Ventures of Citizen Groups by Charles Cagnon. Summer 1982. The NRAG Papers, the Northern Rockies Action Group, 9 Placer Street, Helena, MT 59601.

By far the best investigation of nonprofit organizations operating for-profit businesses. Concise, well written, and thorough. Highly recommended.

9

* *

WHEN NOBODY KNOWS
YOUR NAME

Public relations and publicity

**If you don't like the news, go out and make some of
your own.** —*Scoop Nisker*

Public relations is the great lost opportunity of nonprofit life.
In no other area is it so easy to shine. And yet few tasks receive such a consistently mediocre performance.

Good public relations doesn't require Madison Avenue
hype. It is, quite simply, the bridge between your organization and your community; the informational traffic flows in
both directions. Public relations affects every aspect of your
organizational life. And every one of your staff, Board, and
volunteers is a PR person.

It's Really Publics Relations

"The public" is not a great, seething mass of undifferentiated
humanity. Rather, you're dealing with a highly segmented
group whose various components may have little to do with
each other. The first public to consider is yourself, the inner
circle—your staff, volunteers, and those who know and love
you best. Next might be the people who walk through your
doors to use your services or those who directly benefit from
your work—your clients, members, subscribers, students, pa-
tients. Then there are others who may have heard *something*

about you, but need to know more. And finally, there's the rest of the world: everyone who has yet to receive the message. Your task is to present your story to each of these publics, in a way that is both appealing and relevant.

Of course, the most important asset of any public relations campaign is a compelling organizational mission. If your organization has a clear sense of purpose, then public relations will consist of making sure that it's communicated in all written materials, enlivened by a consistent graphic image, and reflected in the behavior and attitude of everyone involved in the organization.

"Easy for you to say," you may be thinking. "Our brochure's three years old and we can't afford to have it updated. We've dropped two programs and added one. We're critically understaffed. The press hasn't covered us since our big low-income housing demonstration in 1979. And yesterday, we ran out of letterhead!"

And so you wonder: Where do we begin?

BEEFING UP THE BASICS

Organizational image-building takes years to fully achieve. It starts with refocusing your attitude toward the public, and ends with a broad array of graphics, photos, and publicity schemes that tell your story to the world.

Print and Publicity: the Ink and Paper Tools

Everything that your organization prints and distributes is a public relations tool. It builds your image—or undermines it. Thus, quality and consistency can't be overstressed. A good example of this principle is the case of the Urban Community Music Center.

The center sponsors a variety of instrumental music classes, faculty and student concerts, and a number of other special musical activities. They print monthly calendars, fliers announcing events, schedules of classes, a newsletter, and other printed materials. Yet prior to 1982, the publicity for any activity was handled by the staff member who was leading that activity. The result, quite frankly, was a mess. There were no standards of style or format. Tacky, hand-lettered fliers were posted alongside expensive, glossy productions. In their haste, people even neglected essentials such as the date, time, even the music center's name.

Then the center received a grant for a "graphics project." They hired a consultant to analyze their "image" needs. The result was a simple, bold, and flexible style format, which they now adapt to their calendar, newsletter, brochure, special fliers—whatever they need. Typeface, layout, and graphic design remain constant; they copy well even on unsophisticated duplicating machines. Materials from the center are instantly recognizable and leap out from the bulletin board, literature table, or stack of press releases even before they're read. All of the print basics have been covered:

Logo

A logo is a graphic device, unique and easily understandable, which sums up your group to the public. Ideally, it's a design that reproduces well on any standard copying machine. (You should keep on hand a number of camera-ready copies of various sizes for purposes which will inevitably arise.) Unless your group contains someone of unusual talent, *have your logo designed professionally.* When used consistently on all materials, it can provide instant visual recognition while representing the spirit of your group.

Letterhead

Every organization no matter how small or new needs letterhead stationery. It announces that your group is an *entity*, not just a bunch of folks. Select good quality paper, and in the margins feature the name of the executive director and a list of your Board members with affiliations. The typeface should suit your organizational style. Of course, your logo will be prominently displayed. Legal-size envelopes, also printed with your logo and return address, complete the package.

Brochures

Your organizational brochure is your ambassador to the community; it takes your message to places that your small staff could never reach. The exact form of the document requires some thought: Do you need just one, or one for each program? Would specialized brochures reach different audiences for marketing purposes? Does your program brochure fit your fundraising needs? Answer these questions, borrow shamelessly from the brochures of other organizations, and then design your own document. Use:

• Professional typesetting and printing. (No, you cannot get by with typing and photocopying.) For continuity, match the typeface with your letterhead design.

• Attractive graphics, including your logo

• Photos, if possible

• A standard size and format (it will be much cheaper to print) that fits into a legal-size envelope

• Information that won't quickly date. (If you bend this rule, remember that it's better to junk an outdated brochure than to send out bad information.)

How many brochures do you need? Well, how many can you afford? Two thousand copies often cost only a small amount more than one thousand, since the printer's set-up charges constitute the bulk of the price. Before you commit to any numbers, try to carefully estimate your needs. Will you use the brochure in fundraising? How many information requests do you get each year? Are there public locations, such as libraries or community centers, where you can leave stacks of material? Consider all the possible uses of the brochure, and *then* start shopping for printers. Prices commonly vary up to 300 percent. Once your distribution plan has been completed, be relentless about following it up. Nothing is more useless than the dusty unopened boxes of outdated brochures sitting in the storage room, or languishing in the trunk of the executive director's car.

Annual Report

Although an expensive, glossy annual report is often unnecessary, some sort of yearly summation is usually desirable. The document should start off with remarks by the Board president, followed by the executive director's introduction, a clear representation of the financial statement, program summaries, and plans for the next year. Add a few glowing comments by your constituency, and you'll lighten up the whole thing. In most cases, six to eight pages is *plenty*. Use lots of white space; that means no double-page spreads of dense type. Once it's printed, send copies to funders, major donors, friends in the community, and the like. Distribution of the annual report is much narrower than that of the brochure. It's basically an internal document, which you share selectively with the public.

Newsletter

Organizational newsletters can be a real headache. While they're intended to build spirit, image, and a sense of belonging, they often have the opposite effect. Cheap and poorly produced newsletters make organizations appear amateurish, and even the best are expensive to mail. What's more, they take up valuable staff time and energy, while their corresponding impact is difficult to measure. If you already have a newsletter, survey its readers to find out if they read it, what they like, what they don't like, and if they'd be willing to pay to subscribe to it. If you don't have a newsletter now, hold the presses until you complete a mini-marketing survey (see Chapter 8, Survival Tactics) to figure out how it can be useful to your constituency. Given unlimited resources, almost every group could benefit from a relevant and well-written newsletter. Your task is to figure out the priorities.

Public Relations Projects

In addition to the reams of paper and wells of ink that your communications campaign will eventually consume, there are also a number of other tactics that you should consider. Oftentimes these efforts are passed over, even by groups that are relatively sophisticated in their print products. But taken as a whole, the influence of these projects can equal a dozen glossy brochures.

Answering the Phone

For many people, the first contact with your group will be the disembodied voice on the other end of the phone. The quality of this conversation may set the tone for any future relationship with your organization. To illustrate, a cautionary tale . . .

Once there were two museums—the large and prestigious Museum of Modern Art, and the small, unpretentious Folk Art Museum. Now anyone calling the larger organization had her ears assaulted first by aggressive gum chewing, and then by a bored voice intoning: "Museumamodrenart." A request for a specific person was greeted with, "He's out." A request to leave a message met with bored agreement, but the caller generally felt her words had little chance of reaching their destination. It seemed that the organization couldn't care less.

In contrast, the Folk Art Museum phone was answered by the lively voice of a well-trained volunteer saying: "Folk Art Museum, may I help you?" A request for a specific person was met with, "Certainly, may I say who's calling?" And if upon checking, the person happened to be out, the receptionist returned to say, "I'm sorry, Ms. Caller, he's not in, but I expect him back at 3:00. May I leave a message and have him call you?"

Notice the difference. With just a few extra words, the Folk Art receptionist created an impression of professionalism and caring. It takes very little time (and less money) to think through an appropriate phone manner for your group. But it pays off handsomely in good will.

And while we're on the subject of telephones, there's no excuse for an organization to let the public ring endlessly when the office is empty. Purchase an inexpensive answering device to announce your business hours and take messages. It shows that you're on the case even when you're off the job.

Displays

Take a look at the bulletin board in your lobby. Does it contain emergency notices announcing the citizen's action conference in March of 1978? Does it radiate the earnest appeal of your second grade teacher's construction paper cutouts for Back to School Night? Design of the lobby display and bulletin board is a great job for an artistic volunteer. And it's worth a small amount of money spent on typesetting, photo enlargements, and mounting. An attractive portable display board that can be carried with you to speaking engagements is also a terrific investment.

Slide Show or Videotape

Everybody dreams of having one or both of these items—the gorgeous extravaganzas with smooth, professional narration that present your story in a way that no funder could possibly resist. Alas, the more common presentation employs a series of underexposed slides accompanied by the halting voice of an unconfident volunteer. ("This is a classroom scene . . . I know it's a little hard to see, but the children are making Indian masks. Uh, some of the completed masks are hanging on the wall. You could see them better, but the flash didn't work.") Every organization should have fifteen to twenty superb slides that illustrate its work in striking sequence. (Any more than this is boring unless your work naturally lends itself to visuals.) The very best way to get these slides is to have someone on the staff or Board "document" your work, which simply means they show up at activities and snap pictures. They may need to take hundreds of photos to get the required number of good ones. But once you're got them, it's done.

A videotape is another story. It should be undertaken only

if you have very clear evidence that it's absolutely *necessary*. For some reason many groups seem to have a touching faith that a videotape will open the floodgates of grants and public recognition. The truth is that videotapes are only worth doing if they are done well, and that means *expensive*. And of course, once you've produced a videotape, you'll need to buy or frequently rent the equipment to show it. Think this one through with unusual care.

A Speaker's Bureau

A speaker's bureau is a splendid, all-purpose public relations tool which doesn't cost a dime. It's simply a list of people—Board, staff, or volunteers—who are willing to go out into the community and tell your story. Naturally, these people are incredibly charismatic, know your group backwards and forwards, and are not nonplussed by the malfunction of the projector during the slide show. Good opportunities for speakers include meetings of service and social clubs (they may even make a donation to your group), professional associations in related fields, the PTA, church groups, and industry and commercial associations. Inevitably, speakers will cart around some prodigious bundles: brochures, newsletters, fliers advertising your upcoming benefit, the mailing list—and of course, the slide projector and screen.

THEY'VE GOT YOU COVERED. Relations with the Media

You and the media have very different goals: You want coverage; they want news.

Both goals can be met, but you must be willing to do most of the work and play by their rules. Fortunately, these rules are rather simple; and they're not very different from the methods you've employed with funders (see Chapter 6), government officials (see Chapter 10), and other people to whom you market your organization's work.

• *Professionalism*. Every day news writers lay their reputations on the line in cold print. They can't afford to work with someone who doesn't have her facts straight, causes deadline delays, or proves otherwise inept. If you promise a story and don't deliver, you won't get a second chance. Give journalists what they need, and they'll return the favor.

• *Personal contact*. Know who you're dealing with. A visit, lunch, or invitation to tour your facility are all perfectly appropriate. Just as a "funder" is a *person* whose job happens to be distributing money, a "reporter" is a *person* whose job is collecting news. Deal with the person, not the role. On your side, assign one staff member to handle all media contact. Obviously a full-time communications professional would be ideal, but a good job can be done by any personable employee who writes well, thinks on her feet, and isn't afraid to pick up the phone.

• *Easy access*. Playing hard to get is tricky in romance and deadly with the media. Drop everything to talk to the press, return calls immediately, and be *very helpful*. If necessary, you should even bend the rules. Get the reporter a backstage pass, rearrange your class hours for the photographer's convenience, allow the camera crew to sit in on a consultation with a client (with the client's consent, of course).

• *Follow-up*. When you succeed in placing a story, call and thank the writer. It's also thoughtful to drop a note to the editor or station manager to acknowledge coverage, as long as your work isn't controversial. If you are involved in any sort of conflict, it's still appropriate to acknowledge the *fairness* of the reporting.

Breaking into Print

The print and broadcast media gobble up information at an astounding rate. They consume it in gigantic chunks, digest it for the public, and then hunger for more. This insatiable appetite is an advantage for nonprofit organizations: We offer a smorgasbord of options to tempt the media's palate. But first we have to know how to serve up our message.

Learn to Write Press Releases

These are the staple of the media diet. Yet even with dozens of available "how to" manuals and technical assistance workshops, many organizations do not know the basics of constructing and distributing a press release. Herewith, then, one more time, the essential Dos and Don'ts:

ALWAYS:

• Write the press release on your letterhead.

• Put the date and name of *contact person with day and evening phone numbers in the upper right-hand corner*.

• Make sure the contact person is actually available at those numbers for two or three days following the release.

• Center a headline of five or six words in all caps.

• Indent paragraphs five spaces, and double space.

• Limit your releases to two pages or less; type the word "more" at the bottom of the first page, and -30- or ### at the end of the release.

• Put all essential information—the famous five *w*'s (who, what, where, when, and why)—in the first paragraph.

• Place a snappy quote in the second or third paragraph if possible.

• Stick to short paragraphs and short declarative sentences.

• Use a standard last paragraph which sums up your organization.

• Send out a press release whenever you're *doing anything*. "We exist" is not news after the first time, but a new executive director, increased enrollment statistics, a stand you've taken on drug abuse, or even your window display featuring children's art work are all potentially newsworthy.

• Read the newspapers you want to have cover you and write your releases the way their reporters write their stories.

• Follow up with your key contacts.

NEVER:

• Try to be cute, and don't gush. You can't say, "We're brilliant!" But you can quote the mayor if she says it.

• Resort to rhetoric. Copy reading, "Last night at the city

council meeting the small-minded bureaucrats once again showed their indifference to widows and orphans," guarantees your release a one-way trip to the circular file. Be cagier than that: "Last night after the city council meeting, Mr. I.M. Outraged, of the Community Control Lobby, stated that the council members 'once again showed their indifference to widows and orphans by their action to cut emergency spending.'"

• Think that because a release isn't used, it's been wasted. Every thoughtful and well-written press release increases the reporter's understanding of your organization. And what may not be news on the day the space shuttle lands will be cheerfully appreciated on the day the front page story concerns a ribbon-cutting ceremony at the new supermarket.

• Send a release to more than one person at the same paper. Send it to your key contact—then if she doesn't use it, ask who else might be interested.

Make Press Contacts

OK, you've mastered the essentials of a good press release. How do you make certain that it reaches the people who'll display your news in banner headlines? To begin, you construct a press list using the format shown in Table 11.

But where, you may ask, do we find all the papers? By employing the radical method of looking in the Yellow Pages under . . . Newspapers. (If you live in a medium-to-large city, don't reinvent the wheel. Metropolitan areas usually have complete press directories. Contact the United Way if you need help tracking one down.) Call each paper and try to locate the best person to receive your material. Then call him up and introduce yourself. You won't want to hand-address envelopes every time you send out a release. Instead, type your press list onto copier labels and have several sets ready at all times.

Follow That Story

Once your press release is out, you'll need to track its progress. A chart can help (see Table 12).

Table 11 PRESS LIST

PUBLICATION	CONTACTS	LISTINGS/ CALENDAR	OTHER
News & Sun Main St. Red Bluff, CA 94111 555-1212	Don Goodheart/ Features Jane Hardnose/ City Desk	c/o T. Riffic 6 wks. in advance	Can use photos

As you call your press contacts to follow up, try to suggest creative ways that your story might be used. Offer them several story "hooks"—tie-ins to other news events, or an off-beat angle that might appeal to readers. Be helpful, but not pushy. If your contact says he can't use the story, thank him and drop it. Eventually you'll develop a sense about the types of stories that are best for each of your contacts.

Shoot for Features

One good feature article is worth a thousand calendar listings. It showcases your work with greater detail, draws attention to aspects of your organization usually passed over in a news piece, and often includes photographs. Later you can even duplicate the feature and include it as part of your fundraising package. The publicist for a major metropolitan arts organization revealed that at all times he has a list of over a hundred feature story ideas just waiting for the right moment to be pitched. You too should cultivate feature ideas and share them

Table 12 TRACKING CHART

STATION/PUBLICATION	CONTACT	TYPE OF PROGRAM ARTICLE/STORY	REACHED/DATE	RESULT	COMMENTS/FOLLOW-UP
News & Sun	Don G.	features	10/24	will run on community page	called to thank— 10/27
KUBO	Ron T.	PSA Community Bulletin Board	10/24	Calendared 10/27 asked for photo	sent photo 10/25 asked if we could have mention on 28th— will try

regularly with your contacts. Just remember that your part in orchestrating the event to be covered may be difficult and time-consuming. Don't get caught offering a fascinating story that you ultimately can't deliver.

Vary Your Coverage

When news about you does appear, where does it appear? In the City section? The Arts scene? The Social page? Some sections of the paper are worth more than others in terms of readership. The big winner, of course, is the front page. But it's also valuable to simply break out of your usual niche and appear in other sections of the paper. For instance, you could aim for coverage of your fundraising softball tournament as a light feature in the Sports section. Or you might entice the city editor to cover your opening night performance attended by the playwright as hard news, rather than relegating it to the Arts page. Since hardly anyone reads the entire paper, your sudden appearance in an unexpected section will always reach a number of new readers.

Open a Photo File

We all know what a picture is worth—but that's only if it's a good one. Newspapers love to use photographs as long as:

• The activity is genuinely photogenic (two smiling men, unless they're celebrities, won't do)

• The picture is well-exposed, preferably with a light background

• The picture involves action

• No more than three people are included (the exception to this rule is in small town papers where circulation is directly tied to the number of people who get their pictures in the paper)

• Format is at least 5 × 7 glossy (preferably 8 × 10) and all pertinent information (the five w's again) is typed on a label affixed to the back of the picture.

Send Letters to the Editor

This section is one of the best-read pages in the paper, and it can be the perfect place for your organization to break into the news. What about a thoughtful letter from your Board president concerning an item in the news on which your group has taken a stand? Or a letter from one of your constituents praising your work in cleaning up a city park in her neighborhood? This tactic is the salt in your media diet—use sparingly.

Construct a Press Kit

The press kit is the journalist's helper. It makes his job easier and your story more accessible. It's usually handed to media workers attending a performance, press conference, or other staged event. Every organization should have the makings of a press kit, though not everyone will often use it. The kit includes:

- A press release on the specific activity or program
- Several good photos, properly labeled
- An organizational brochure
- An annual report
- A list of Board members with affiliations

Put all this information together in a slim, light-weight folder. Groups that use press kits frequently, such as performing arts companies, often have folders specially made with their logo printed on the front.

Cracking the Airwaves

Strategies for the broadcast media are not much different from the methods you use with print journalists. However, there are a few twists and a few different options for coverage.

The Public Service Announcement

This useful little item (often called a PSA) is really just a press release for the broadcast media. Unlike the press release, however, it is written to be read aloud, and must be timed to fit the individual station's needs. The standard time limits are ten, twenty, thirty, and sixty seconds. Format on the page is the same as for the press release with the addition of the words, "Timed—20 seconds" written at the bottom. Listen to your local radio stations to see what they use and when they use it. Make your PSA fit their format. Writing PSAs is an exercise in getting down to essentials; with only ten seconds of airtime, there's no time for padding.

The PSA is your entree to the broadcaster, but often the station will offer a number of other possibilities for getting out your story:

- Local news programs
- Call-in shows
- Interview shows
- Daily calendars
- Free speech messages
- Editorial replies

You'll attempt to interest the people involved in each of these areas by following the same format you use with newspapers, including the same careful personal contact and follow-up. Adapt your press list to reflect the programming options of broadcasting (see Table 13).

TWELVE MONTHS A YEAR. The Annual Publicity Cycle

As with fundraising, your public relations and media campaign should be planned over the course of the year to enable proper budgeting of both time and money. Get a big calendar, one that lets you see the entire year in a single scan and leaves plenty of room in the margins for notes. Then ask: When do we most need coverage?

You might answer:

- During the annual fundraising drive
- Around our awards ceremony
- When we release our Clean Air Index
- Just before our annual benefit

Target these events on the calendar; they're the major

Table 13 PROGRAMMING LIST

STATION	POTENTIAL PROGRAMMING	PSA	LEAD TIME/CONTACTS
KUBD	Nightly News: 7:30 PM Jim Drylook	:30 copy	Stacey Traffic 2 weeks in advance
KPJK	AM Brown County Coverage 9–10 AM local issues; submit ideas to producer Fred Brown for circulation	:10 :20 :30 throughout day	ATTN: County Affairs (3 weeks in advance) Call Rosie to make sure its calendared

focus of your campaign. Estimate your lead time, list all materials needed for each campaign, and budget their costs. Set targets for coverage and keep records of what you do so that evaluation can be built in to each campaign.

It's important to balance your annual schedule between long-term image-building activities (such as drawing feature coverage of your work, refining the slide show, or talking a local cable station into making a professional broadcast PSA), and the short-term marketing activities needed to publicize your specific programs and events.

NO NEWS IS BAD NEWS, But Bad News Is Worse News

Eventually every organization receives bad press. Your programs are criticized, your director gets caught with his hand in the till, your candidate loses big, your workers go on strike charging discrimination, your artistic director is called a second-rate talent by the local newspaper's second-string critic. What do you do?

First, don't overreact. Sometimes it's better to just let a dig from the press slide rather than mobilize all forces. Make sure you don't unintentionally draw more attention to the bad news. This is particularly true in the case of bad reviews for arts organizations. The best defense in these cases is usually the proverbial good offense: Counter bad news with good news in another area. By its very nature news is ephemeral. No matter how bad it is, you can ride it out if your organization is strong.

If the issue isn't going to go away, then a response may be necessary. Think through the situation with your staff. Examine the ramifications of each response, then *as quickly as possible* deliver to your best press contacts the *minimum information possible*. This will be the "company line," which you'll amplify whenever you must, keeping in mind that old World War II adage: Loose lips sink ships.

The organization must speak with one voice. And only one

person should be issuing press statements. That person is the communications staffer, not the president of the Board. (Ironically, the only time it's appropriate for an organizational quote to come from your PR person is in a "bad news" crisis.) Don't lose your reputation for honesty and dependability because of one bad story or exposé. Journalists are professionals. You can't expect them to ignore genuine news just because it's your bad news. But it's during a bad news situation that you'll most depend upon your relationships with media professionals to assure that coverage is fair, even if it's not what you'd choose to have reported.

Of course, there are many problems that even the most impeccable press relations won't solve. Financial scandal, organizational ineptitude, and bad programming cannot be blamed on media coverage; they're your problems, and you'll need to deal with them in a forthright manner before you can once again expect the kind of coverage that you desire. In these moments, the best thing that good media relationships can do is give you a slight buffer of indulgence which may enable you to repair your problems before they balloon into a worse public embarrassment.

HOW TO TELL WHEN YOU'VE MADE IT

Unfortunately, as far as publicity and public relations are concerned, you've never made it. You'll always be striving to keep your organization's name and accomplishments headlined in the news and fresh in people's minds. But that shouldn't surprise anyone who works for a nonprofit. None of our work is ever done.

ADDITIONAL RESOURCES

Strategy for Access to Public Service Advertising by Glenn Hirsch and Alan Lewis. 1976. Public Media Center, 25 Scotland Street, San Francisco, CA 94133.

One of the best practical guides for nonprofit groups determined to enhance their public profile through the media.

Media How-To Notebook. Media Alliance, Fort Mason Building D, San Francisco, CA 94123.

An excellent step-by-step primer to gaining exposure in both print and broadcast media. Even an experienced publicist can learn from this intelligent and pragmatic guide.

Presenting Performances by Thomas Wolfe. 1981. American Council for the Arts, 570 Seventh Avenue, New York, NY 10018.

There is no better available handbook to organizing and publicizing performances and special events for small organizations.

The Publicity Handbook by David R. Yale. 1982. Bantam Books, New York, NY.

For the money, this thorough, well-written paperback is your best guide to nonprofit publicity.

10

* *

FINESSING CITY HALL

Coalitions, lobbying, and the question of power

> Every kind of public work involves desire for some kind of power. . . . The only man totally indifferent to power is the man totally indifferent to his fellow men.
> —*Bertrand Russell*

We have to get smart about power. For too long, it's been a dirty word in the nonprofit sector—a disturbing force always held by others that seldom seems to work in our favor. Generally, we misunderstand power. Unfortunately, our fears and misperceptions often lead us to act and sound like the Timid Sector.

"I run the other way when someone starts talking politics," says the executive director of a metropolitan youth agency. "Our organization serves hundreds of kids—all from different families, different neighborhoods and backgrounds. The last thing we need is to start taking sides in some local dispute. After all, our job is to operate in the *public* interest."

True enough. But there are times when the broad public interest served by your organization will conflict with more limited special interests within the community. Your goal to build an inner city playground may be blocked by developers. Your community clinic may meet opposition from private doctors. Your free food distribution program may collide with red tape, zoning laws, and city bureaucrats.

And if you can't seize, borrow, or attract power, you're sunk.

MODIFIED MACHIAVELLIANISM. Politics for Nonprofits

"We know what happens to people who stay in the middle of the road," one experienced nonprofit organizer told us. "They get run over." And in a phrase, that's what nonprofit politicking is all about. We usually enter the political realm because we have no other options. But when we do it right, we can find our reluctant expeditions productive.

Effectiveness

Power is energy harnessed in the pursuit of specific ends. "Our Board used to be very nervous about ruffling anyone's feathers," remembers one staff member for a community recycling center. "And as a result, we never got what we needed from the city government. Then we lucked into this new Board president fresh from the corporate world. And during our next conflict with the city manager's office, he just called in some favors with a few well-placed phone calls. Nothing heavy, but very much to the point. We won, and nobody seemed to hold a grudge. It was a good lesson."

Protection

Unless our groups are specifically engaged in social action, we turn to politics only as a last resort. This is often the case when our very existence is threatened. "Our landlord was going to sell our building right out from underneath us," said the executive director of a performing arts agency. "We couldn't afford to buy it, like they were pressuring us to do. So we did the only thing left: We called upon everyone we knew in the community with influence to make a pitch on our behalf. Then we asked them to ask *their* friends to do the same. By the time we were done, we had lined up dozens of well-regarded people in our corner—and our landlord eventually lost his interest in selling."

Commitment

Sometimes, despite the pain and anxiety involved in any political bout, we discover that the experience has clarified our convictions and renewed our commitment. That which has not killed us has made us stronger. Harry C. Boyte, a social theorist who has examined successful activist organizations, writes that people must "develop the self-consciousness, skills, knowledge, and confidence to challenge those in control of their destinies." On many levels, that's the very thing we're trying to encourage.

If We Win, Who Loses: the Art of Strategic Thinking

Of course, you can also go overboard. Some nonprofit workers get an unaccustomed taste of influence and develop an insatiable appetite. They attend endless meetings. They organize irrelevant coalitions. And they soon discover that amateur politicking is sometimes nothing more than a conspiracy to waste time.

Politics can also be very dangerous. Too many novices introduce their opinions into all manner of controversy; they aim to win new friends even as they stir up a hornet's nest of unnecessary enemies. They fail to think strategically.

In essence, strategic thinking is merely recognition of the political context. None of us operate in a vacuum. We're surrounded by other forces, almost all of them larger, richer, more powerful, and probably shrewder and more ruthless than we are. Strategic thought can help balance the score.

"We spent months trying to figure out who would oppose our move into the neighborhood," confided the director of a new group home for developmentally disabled adults. "We spoke with people individually, and tried to figure out what they feared and what they thought they stood to lose. Then we countered with solid information, statistics, and anecdotes about places where similar arrangements were very successful. When a few people finally came over to our side, we got them talking to their neighbors. And by the time the issue went public, there weren't many people who wanted to stand up and object to our presence with what by then appeared to be sheer ignorance and bigotry."

In every successful political action, you'll need to ask the same kinds of questions:

• Who are our natural allies? What do they stand to gain? How can we enlist their aid?

• Who is directly or even indirectly affected by what we're attempting? Can we include them? Who needs to learn our plans first *from us* (not the grapevine or the newspapers)? Funders? Other organizations? The media?

• If we win, who loses? Are there people who would usually support us, who might oppose us in this particular instance? Can their opposition be eliminated, deflected, or softened?

• Who are our natural adversaries? What are their resources? Their reputation? Can we beat them?

• Will they oppose us publicly? Is this an advantage or disadvantage?

• Who are the opposition's friends? What kind of help will they lend? Can we turn their friendship into a liability?

• Where is the money? Who gives it, gets it, and touches it along the way?

• And finally, most importantly, is there any way in which our conflict can be resolved so that everybody feels they have emerged as a winner—or at least, not as a loser?

WHEN 2 + 2 = 5. The Logic and Influence of Alliances

All this suggests one of the most powerful political tools at your disposal: interorganizational alliances. Unfortunately, most nonprofit workers tend to think of alliances only in their most rigid or fragile forms. Perhaps they've had experience

with hastily constructed electoral coalitions or do-nothing professional associations. And they rightly resist the impulse to
further complicate their own organizations with the bureaucratic baggage of an unproven ally.

The best alliances are those which arise organically among
the people of compatible organizations. You discover one another at a conference and find that although your service areas
are different, you have many common concerns. Or you attend a City Planning Commission meeting to testify on the
need for a playground in the neighborhood and you're im-
pressed by another organization's testimony on the lack of
shelter for the homeless. When this occurs, don't lose these
people; *make organizational friends.*

If you want to build a relationship with a new organization, then try supporting their efforts. Attend their benefits.
Comment upon the aspects of their work that you genuinely
admire. Share a beer, a meal, or a couple of hours of casual
conversation outside the office with leaders of the other group.
The personal and social can then become political in the best
sense of the word. Then figure out what you'd like to accomplish by asking such questions as:

What do you want from the relationship?

There should be a specific reason for joining forces, even
informally. Your alliance will require time and effort; why
squander it if there's no payoff? That's not to say that the rewards must always be immediate. You may find that you'll
benefit several years from now from relationships informally
constructed today.

One good reason for forming alliances is to build your own
organization or to borrow credibility from a larger, more powerful cousin. And that means that you must wisely select your
allies. Do your prospective partners really have anything to
offer besides goodwill? Do they enjoy the kind of reputation
that you would like to have? Are your constituencies in agreement—at least on the issue that unites your groups for the
moment? (Beware of depending on a group weaker and more
disorganized than your own. Alliances are all about the con-

centration of strength and power, not the mutual compatibility of shared defects.)

Is the alliance really a substitute for building your own operational base?

Shortcuts are always tempting. How easy it would be if you only had to latch onto the coattails of a more developed organization in order to establish your own base of power. But it doesn't work that way. Alliances only prosper when everyone involved brings to the conference table some tangible resource. There should be no free rides.

That means you'll be expected to have built (and continue to build) your own constituency. If you fail to do so, you simply can't be trusted. Nor can your erstwhile allies. For in the end, the people who walked through the door with your new partners will probably walk out again when they leave. Solid base-building is the prerequisite for any serious political action. It's a lazy and ultimately ineffective organization that tries to skip the first step.

How deeply do you want to be committed?

There are several levels of association. The most modest relationship may consist of nothing more than a public endorsement. The next step might be an informal agreement to work together on a specific issue. From there, organizations may wed themselves to long-term coalitions built around actions, visions, or areas of service. The point is that you should know what your'e getting yourself into—and for how long and how deeply. Of course, you must consider the future ramifications of your present commitment. There are risks in even a simple endorsement if it pigeonholes you in one camp or another. But in some cases nothing short of a formal declaration of a united front will be effective. Finally, you'll only be able to measure the risks of any alliance when you're absolutely certain about what it is that you hope to achieve.

How to Cultivate Alliances

In the hardball world of politics, most of us will never be anything other than an occasional pinch hitter. But that's another reason why we need to perfect our skill at acquiring appropriate allies: The motto of the opposition will always be, Divide and conquer.

Actually, most of us are on solid ground here. If there's been any progress in our organizations, then for years we've probably been building informal relationships within our community. We know something about strategic friendships. If we were to codify our best instincts, we'd probably end up talking about the following.

Compatible Self-interest

Our natural allies probably won't share our specific interest in any one issue. After all, they have different histories as well as different strengths, personalities, and problems. The best partners will have their own reasons for wanting friends; they'll need us, as we need them, and from there, we'll hammer out the terms of our mutual survival pact.

Limited Goals and Discernable Limits

Most alliances aren't lifetime arrangements. Of course, we should always maintain friendly, cooperative ties with other community groups; but our strategic relationships—the deals cut to get something in return—are usually intense, informal, and short-lived. If they're to be successful, they must also be clearly constructed. From the start, you should establish the ground rules: Who has decision-making authority within each organization? Who speaks for the alliance? What information can be made public, and when? If financial transactions are involved, who'll handle them? How will the bills be paid? These matters can't be solved through simple goodwill. The failure to deal with them early on will inevitably result in resentment and sidetrack any future collaboration.

The Value of Little Victories

The best alliances start small. Pick a modest goal, and make sure you can deliver your end of the bargain. Do it right and do it on schedule. Once you've proven yourself (and checked out the reliability of your prospective partner), you can then start thinking about more important and more complicated efforts.

LOBBYING. The Why and How of Influence

In the nonprofit imagination, probably no political activity is so persistently misperceived as lobbying. And with good cause. To the general public, lobbyists remain the bad guys of politics—shadow figures of special interest wielding influence and stacking favors against the commonweal. "You can't use tact with a Congressman," a presidential cabinet member advised writer Henry Adams. "A Congressman is a hog. You must take a stick and hit him on the snout."

The bribe and bully school of influence has led many people to believe that lobbying is somehow inappropriate, immoral, and perhaps even illegal within the nonprofit sector. The fact is, lobbying is simply mishandled and misunderstood.

The term itself hails back to the notion of good citizens standing outside the halls of government—in the lobby—waiting for an opportunity to collar an official and color his opinion. Lobbying is persuasion. In common practice, the lobbyist sets his sights upon legislators, government appointees, civil servants, or other decision-makers. Nonprofit groups, like other special interests, undertake a lobbying campaign when they find themselves in need. Perhaps it's a bill that must be passed or defeated, a point of view that needs to be articulated from the high offices of government, or even a bid for preferential treatment. In any case, the nonprofit lobbyist aims for a specific goal. But in addition to getting what you desire, there are also several other benefits accrued through the lobbying process.

Visibility

A successful lobbying effort, even when conducted with discretion and a minimum of public contact, can create the impression that you have been graced with the power to influence others. And a reputation for being politically astute stemming from a modest victory can be turned into a tool for building alliances with people and organizations who really *do* wield political clout. To return to our modified Machiavellianism, being taken seriously by those in power as a force to be reckoned with is more important than the fate of any specific issue.

Political Realism

Immersion in the political process is a sobering experience for anyone who still believes that the rapids of public life are best run in the sturdy boat of good intentions. In launching a lobbying effort, you'll quickly learn what people think about your organization. You'll be asking for favors, testing limits, and pushing the boundaries of the possible. In the end, win or lose, you'll emerge with greater clarity about your organization's relationship to the community at large and the people who make the decisions.

Contacts

Lobbying forces you to finally take an interest in the issues that stir hearts and minds beyond the doors of your own organization. Out of necessity, you'll investigate your community's power structure; you'll explore—at first tentatively and from a safe distance—the factions and rivalries that make life interesting and deadly for the political players. Over time, you'll build personal relationships with staff and officials that can be nurtured in the less turbulent days ahead. Best of all, your organization will acquire a definite shape in the eyes of the decision-makers. You'll distinguish yourself from the countless other "worthwhile organizations" who march to the bench in an endless parade of righteousness and need. By taking action that is appropriate, planned, and disciplined, you'll become authentic in the political realm.

Enter the IRS

We're all aware that the First Amendment of the U.S. Constitution guarantees every citizen the right "to petition the government for a redress of grievances." Yet in the life of a 501(c)3 nonprofit organization—the most common IRS designation for tax-exempt groups—these rights have been qualified. Nonprofits may lobby, but there are limitations. Exceed the limitations, and you can lose your tax-exempt status.

Until 1976, the IRS forbade lobbying as a "substantial part of an organization's activities" if the organization was a nonprofit. This vague and perilous phrase discouraged many organizations from lobbying at all. They feared to step over the invisible line and lose their precious tax exemption, as could easily happen to any group even temporarily pivoting to an activist role.

Since 1976, nonprofits have been able to elect for an objective test by filing Form 5768, "Election/Revocation of Election by an Eligible Section 501(c)3 Organization to Make Expenditures to Influence Legislation." The good news is that Form 5768 is far easier to complete than the cumbersome and convoluted federalese might imply.

According to the objective test, nonprofit organizations can spend 20 percent of their first $500,000 on lobbying. From this amount, 15 percent may be allocated to direct lobbying; that is, letters, phone calls, and visits directly intended to influence legislators and decision-makers. The remaining 5 percent must be spent on grass roots lobbying, or efforts mounted to urge your constituency to lobby in your behalf. If you exceed the limitation in any one year, you'll be subject to a 25 percent excise tax. Sail above the limit by 150 percent over a four-year period, and you'll lose your tax exemption. In any situation, you may lobby to influence legislation, but never to elect or defeat a candidate for public office.

If you plan to lobby as a primary activity, then you should probably explore an alternative tax status for your group. The 501(c)4 "Civic Leagues and Welfare Organizations" designation will allow you to lobby without limitation. But while you'll remain free from corporate income taxes, the donations made to your organization will no longer be exempt. Some organizations establish separate corporate entities to cover lobbying, thus separating their fragile tax-exempt, tax-deductible services from the knottier matter of influence peddling. In any case, you should seek legal advice (and IRS counsel) should you plan to engage in a substantial amount of lobbying. Ignorance of the law, as they're fond of saying in federal court, is no excuse.

How to Lobby: the Three-Step Approach

Now that you know why you should lobby and what to watch out for, it's time to get down to the nuts and bolts of practical action. Probably the best advice to any beginning lobbyist is to seek the protective wing of a more experienced player. Here you'll learn the ropes in a way that can't be taught in books. You'll get a sense of the game. And you'll learn about the individuals who wield power in your own community. Barring that, you can gradually develop your lobbying finesse by carefully considering the following steps.

Planning—Everything You Should Do Before They Learn What You're Up To

Know Your Issue Learn the various angles of each argument. Become as familiar with your opponent's position as your own. Frame your argument in terms of facts and figures. "Little children are suffering" is not as powerful as "60 percent of the children under twelve in the Longwood neighborhood do not get even one adequate meal each day." Then double-check all the facts and figures. Remember to think strategically: Who wins? Who loses? Who cares? Who pays?

Know the Process Political action often involves a maze of procedural problems, clearly intended to bedevil the novice. For example, the introduction of legislation may involve a number of complicated tasks such as tracking your bill through a briar patch of committees, while simultaneously pursuing a half-dozen legislators. Even a relatively simple matter, like addressing the City Council during a public meeting, may require advance knowledge of the rules and procedures to insure that you get your turn. Before you ever appear in public, make certain that you know how the game is played. Ask questions of staff, accessible officials, and more experienced nonprofit lobbyists.

Know the Decision-makers　Start by researching the voting records of the decision-makers. Identify alliances and factions. If Representative Garcia votes for your proposal, does that mean Representatives Jones and Washington will automatically oppose it? Get a handle on the personal idiosyncracies that so often affect decisions. Family histories and underlying emotional connections will often counter a politician's partisan interests and produce aid from unexpected corners.

Use the System　Most elected officials employ several smart, informed, capable staff people who will help you out if you can pose your issue so that it reflects well upon their boss. Assistance can come in the form of inside tips, introductions, or even phone calls and photocopying. Hired professionals, such as lawyers, budget analysts, and administrators, may also play a role. Cultivate them if you can. But recognize the crucial difference between their role as civil servants and the distinctly political, and thus assailable, forces governing the decisions of elected officials.

Approach—How You Should Appear to the Decision-Makers

Demonstrate Wide Community Support　Almost every organization claims to speak for a broad base of the community. But hardly any of us really do. In lobbying, we're concerned mainly with the *appearance* of diverse support. Or to borrow a phrase from Kare Anderson, the California-based trainer of citizen lobbyists, we must "cut deals with unlikely allies."

When your lobbying team walks into the mayor's office, you should broadly represent the stereotypes of class, sex,

race, age, occupation, and political affiliation that might logically gather around your issue. Never mind that you've never
worked together before and you don't agree on any other
point. For the moment you're allies aimed at achieving a single goal. Just consider which group is more formidable: three
very similarly dressed white working women in their mid-thir-
ties lobbying with obvious self-interest for a day-care center?
Or the unlikely troika of a white middle-aged male banker, a
young Chicana blue-collar mother, and an elderly black man
representing the neighborhood organization that will welcome
the day-care onto its block?

Select Favorable Turf   The advantage always goes to the
home team. If you can persuade the decision-maker to meet in
your office, then you've already implicitly established the legitimacy of your group. You can better your position by making certain that during the meeting your organization hums
with activity, while the fabled cross section of the community
scurries about your office.

Map Out the Strategy and Keep Score   It's essential to
get your story straight. And this can be difficult when in the
middle of a lobbying effort your story necessarily begins to
change. Commit your strategies to paper and then share them
only with the people involved in the effort. (Even a campaign
run with integrity can come back to haunt you if you're sloppy
about names and favors.) Still, you must maintain records on
who is contacting which official, when the meeting occurred,
and what commitment, if any, resulted from the effort. Within
six weeks, you'll need these records to jog your memory and
keep track of your progress. Remember, it's worse than embarrassing to ask a favor from somebody who already rendered
it two weeks ago.

Lobby as a Team to Get Commitments   Limit your lobbying group to a manageable size—three is usually plenty. Know
what you're going to say, who's going to say it, and when. In

other words: Plan, rehearse, and role-play the encounter. The essence of your position should be powerfully and clearly compressed to be accessible even to a distracted official during a ten-second conference in the hallway. And remember why you're there: not to shake hands, not to provide information, but to secure a commitment on a particular action.

Don't Take No for an Answer In politics, almost every decision is eventually subject to change given the proper combination of time, pressure, influence, and approach. Take the long view. Even after a loss, position your organization to renew the struggle after the next election or turnover in commissioners. Nothing speaks as loudly to elected officials as the genuine and unflagging commitment of those who voted them into office and have the power to vote them out.

Follow-up—How to Secure Your Victory and Prepare for the Future

Thank Everyone Involved Show your appreciation for the hard work and wisdom of the decision-makers who supported you. If there's an opportunity, thank them in public. For allies in more sensitive positions, such as media workers or civil servants, you'll discover that discretion is the better part of appreciation. Here a simple phone call will demonstrate your good intentions (and good manners), while keeping the lines open for future collaboration.

Stay Connected Keep close to the people who've helped you out and from whom you'll undoubtedly need help again. People with leverage and clout belong on your mailing list, at your public functions, and on your Board. In particular, keep the decision-makers informed about your successes so that they can take credit for supporting you. You're golden if everyone feels that they've gained in some small way by associating with you.

Stay Informed After an initial foray into the political realm, you may be tempted to quickly withdraw before your luck runs out or before you take another licking. That's fine. There's no need to play politics for the sake of playing. Other people, talented amateurs, will do that for you. They'll be your primary resource for hard facts, gossip, predictions, and advice of varying quality. Your best move is to return to your relationship with the old-timer who can boast (but doesn't) of his connections, history, and a fistful of favors accrued over three decades of local politicking. Buy the newspapers, read the war stories, and remember the names and faces. If you're going to continue to battle in the political world, you'll need to stay smart.

ADDITIONAL RESOURCES

Cutting Deals with Unlikely Allies: An Unorthodox Approach to Playing the Political Game by Kare Anderson. 1981. Anderson Negotiations/Communications Press, 600 Athol Avenue, Oakland, CA 99610.

Kare Anderson's sharp, witty, sanguine advice and strategies are a must for the citizen lobbyist. This is clearly the most useful (and most entertaining) guide available for inexperienced nonprofit groups now playing the political game to win.

How You Can Influence Congress: The Complete Handbook for the Citizen Lobbyist by George Alderson and Everett Sentman. 1979. E. P. Dutton, New York, NY.

This guide focuses upon congressional lobbying, though the examples and advice can be adapted to local politics. Extremely thorough and well written.

"Coalitions and Other Relations" by Tim Sampson. *The Organizer,* Fall 1983. The Institute for Social Justice, 628 Baronne, New Orleans, LA 70113.

In four smart pages, Tim Sampson summarizes the potential and problems of organizational alliances, particularly as
they apply to social action organizations. People interested in
the technique and theory of community organizing and other
nonprofit political tools might consider subscribing to the excellent (and inexpensive) quarterly journal in which the
Sampson article appears.

11

* *

EXPANSION AND EXTINCTION
Growth, mergers, and calling it quits

> There is nothing permanent, except change.
> —*Heraclitus*

It's called organizational vertigo.

You finally manage to put the financial records in order, and then two months later the new office computer consigns your efforts to the trashbin of bookkeeping history. You build solid alliances with the local shakers and movers, only to watch them flounder in bankruptcy court, lose their re-elections, or pull up stakes and leave town. You've just about got it all figured out—the finer points of program evaluation, the subtle mysteries of management, the vast and varied skills, contacts, postures, and positions that ensure nonprofit glory. And then everything changes.

The fact is you don't know whether to alter your goals, redouble your efforts, or walk away and let it die.

It's a common dilemma, an inevitable part of your organizational destiny. Decisions must be made.

THE TEMPTATIONS OF GROWTH

This is a story about coming of age.

For more than twenty years, the Hesperian Foundation in

Palo Alto, California, has successfully challenged conventional wisdom about health care in the Third World. Instead of dispatching American medical teams to remote villages in Latin America and Africa, the organization now seeks to educate, equip, and ultimately empower the villagers themselves. With a paid staff of six and an annual budget of about $300,000, the Hesperian Foundation has published *Where There Is No Doctor*, a practical guide for the diagnosis and treatment of common health ailments written in simple language and highlighted by evocative illustrations. Today *Where There Is No Doctor* has been translated into twenty-six different language editions, and several million copies have been distributed.

Of course, in the early days, no funder would touch the organization's radical concept of public health and patient treatment. For one thing, it entirely bypassed the medical establishment. And foundations, while they have a history of contributing generously to medical research and hospitals, are not generally known for supporting risky, controversial projects which suggest that a simple handbook is better than sixteen years of schooling. But the organization struggled on. (For a time, the founder even lived in a tree house.) And as the Hesperian Foundation's accomplishments emerged as a model for other health care organizations, its grant applications began hitting 1,000 percent. Eventually, foundations approached *them*. New ideas for similar, valuable projects became plentiful.

Money was available; temptation to expand was almost irresistible.

So they sat down, discussed the merits and problems of expansion, and decided to resist it. *They decided not to grow.* Their primary work, they believed, would become diluted if they were to increase their workload. The democratic, self-help nature of the organization would buckle under the weight of additional staff, inevitable bureaucratization, and the loss of control over their product. "In our utopia," says Michael Blake, Hesperian's administrative director, "we would wither away."

The Hesperian Foundation is an unusual organization. But what's most striking about the group is the *consciousness* with which its Board and staff decided to stay the course. For in the ordinary life of most nonprofit organizations, these essential questions are seldom asked: Do we grow, combine, decline, or close up shop? And what happens if we dare to ignore the question altogether?

Bigger or Better?

The truth is that most organizational growth proceeds not from planning or need, but as a triumph of inertia over logic, demand, and human benefit.

For most nonprofits, like their profit-making relatives, big has always been better. And why not? Surely, if we are doing our job, the world could benefit from more of our services. And anyway, isn't growth a law of nature?

Money

Organizations grow because money is available for new projects, staff, and buildings. And money is always accompanied by its own logic. ("If we had to work so hard to raise the $10,000 for our new office, then we must really need it.") Or some unlikely benefactor will make your dreams come true by actually offering cold cash if you undertake their pet project. The dream swiftly changes into a nightmare when you discover that the project has little to do with the true purpose of your organization and only impedes progress toward your duly stated goals. In the parlance of big government critics, this is called "throwing money at problems." And of course, it's extremely difficult to throw it back.

Prestige

The attractions of status are somewhat more slippery. Imagine that you run an agency with forty employees. Does that mean that you handle twice the responsibility and get twice the results as the manager supervising a staff of twenty? Probably not. But upon this dubious equation, many people balance their careers, budgets, and dreams. Rest assured that administrators and Boards primarily interested in personal position will always prove friendly to the implied honors of growth. In a more reasonable world, we might remember that the word "prestige" derives from a Latin root meaning "conjuror's trick" or "illusion" and, better yet, that the French derivative refers to a "blindfold."

Power

Power also has its price. To illustrate: For years, organizers of a small urban mental health clinic found themselves at odds with their city's administrators and local officials. Each year, when funding was reviewed, they'd drag themselves into the council chambers and make the familiar plea for funds. Each year the city fathers would wag their heads, red-pencil their proposal, and send them out of the room with a fraction of their request. When the federal government awarded the clinic a $2 million in-service training contract, they suddenly found they had new friends. City officials wanted to work with the clinic in order to train municipal employees. Council members began taking credit for their longstanding support of the organization. And finally, the clinic found that it now had sufficient power to wrest a larger share of its funding request from the city budget. The only problem was that the new in-service training program absorbed almost all of the agency's time and staff. And the quality of the original services, for which the clinic was known and respected, rapidly declined.

Good Growth

All of this is not to say that growth is bad. Oftentimes expansion is essential; part of your mandate. But it also requires a very sharp eye to make the distinction between added muscle and a malignant tumor. Take for example, the Farralones Institute.

In the 1970s, a handful of countercultural technocrats banded together to form the Farralones Institute, an educational organization aimed at nothing less than the reformation of community life. In their rural haven in Occidental, California, they pioneered a model for an ecologically sound, energy efficient social organization, right down to the waste management systems. Through the years, interns joined the communards to pick up the latest developments in wind, water, and solar energy. In no time, the Farralones Institute became the nation's leading experiential think tank for "appropriate" technology.

Then in 1979, they encountered their first crisis of plenty. The Peace Corps awarded the organization a large training contract. And suddenly the opinions of people living outside the community became important. "We had to deal with the problem of whether the government officials would see us as a sixties commune or a group of highly skilled trainers," said one staff member. The population of the community mushroomed from a half-dozen permanent members to more than thirty trainees. The purpose of community life quickly shifted to teaching the intricacies of solar food drying, fuel efficient cookstoves, and peddle or treddle powered machinery—all slated for the Third World.

Was this growth harmful to the organization?

No. While the Farralones Institute moved away from its original character as a community bent on research and development, the larger goals of the organization were furthered by the Peace Corps contract. Growth provided an opportunity to spread working knowledge of appropriate technology throughout corners of the world that would have never otherwise been touched by the work of the institute.

Growth, finally, has very little to do with institutional needs. It must always be evaluated in terms of organizational mission: Will expansion (or for that matter, contraction) help us to improve the quality of our work?

THE GREAT COMPROMISE. Reorganizations and Mergers

None of us can avoid growing and shrinking pains. It's the nature of organizational life—crawling until we can walk, stumbling through adolescence, striding toward maturity. So it's only natural that at the height of a crisis, someone on the Board will strike a parental attitude by suggesting reorganization. Generally, they'll mean that something fundamental has to change, but they usually can't (or won't) say what.

An emotional plea for decisive action often sounds both bold and vague enough to appeal to many Board members. (This is also a favorite euphemism for "We really need to get rid of some people.") Thus, an organization will plunge into several months of action and reaction that closely resemble life in a Cuisinart.

Of course, there is nothing wrong with changing programs, swapping procedures, and even switching around staff once you know where you're heading. But beware the old ploy of obscuring the need for essential and possibly painful change by applying an inessential poultice of reorganization. The truth is that reorganization often serves as a substitute for real change. "Reorganization," declares Robert Townsend, writing about the corporate world, "should be undergone about as often as major surgery. And should be as well planned and as swiftly executed." Otherwise, there's trouble ahead. . . .

• An organization is racked with dissension and plagued by the dwindling productivity of its staff. The Board steps in, changing some job descriptions and instituting a new system for settling employee grievances. But they fail to consider the underlying question: Has the executive mishandled his duties, and should he be replaced?

• Earned income levels have substantially fallen over a three-year period. Alarmed by the growing deficit, the Board hires a new development director and commits to an expanded program of fundraising. Once again, reorganization screens the real dilemma: No one seems to know whether a market still exists for the organization's services.

• A financial crisis prompts the Board to declare that no new programs will be introduced until the organization accumulates a small cash reserve. A hiring freeze is instituted. Current programs are cut back 25 percent. Without the benefit of a formal declaration, the organization has now changed its fundamental purpose from service to survival. But they fail to ask the real question: Is the price we pay worth the reduction in our ability to serve the community?

Mergers for Strength and Survival

In the nonprofit world, we assume that our efforts are unique. We're intimate with that curious blend of ideals, goals, history, and people that gives our work meaning. Understandably, we're convinced that another organization would mix with our own like water and oil. Such are the vanities of our sector.

In fact, mergers can remedy managerial and financial ills that have plagued an organization for years. And while many groups seek the shelter of a stronger one when they are in trouble, the merger process can also add power and resources to an already-sturdy organization. So for a moment put aside your visions of corporate conglomerates, unfriendly takeovers, and social service monopolies, and consider the three major benefits that characterize a practical merger:

Program Potential

You share aspirations, similar programs, and a vision of the world as it should be. Why not share offices? In fact the best mergers usually combine organizations that might otherwise consider themselves rivals. You should combine with the organizations whose staff, plans, and programs you'd love to steal. When Accountants for the Public Interest in Rhode Island merged with The Support Center network across the country, the smaller organization found that it soon enjoyed greater credibility, an increased public profile, and access to the skills of a substantially larger staff. "It felt good to be part of a larger, well-organized whole," said the director of the new center.

Leadership

Some organizations merge in search of a leader. They surrender their caseloads, programs, and obligations to a more efficient body and then breathe a sigh of relief. And oddly enough, there seems to be little conflict over who runs the new organization. The Greater New York Fund/United Way surveyed a number of merged organizations and found that "there never appears to have been any question as to who would be the executive director of the merged agency. To the contrary, the existence of recognized leadership qualities in an executive was often one of the features that made the merger desirable." Of course, this enviable lack of conflict is less likely to be found among organizations that feel themselves pressed by fiscal crisis into the arms of a larger group. But in the best cases, the leaders of the new group will stand for stability and direction, rather than authority and control.

Funding and Fiscal Management

Mergers should prove the old adage that two can live as cheaply (or at least, as efficiently) as one. To begin, there may be a reduction in overhead. The combined organization won't need to hire two bookkeepers, pay two rents, or use two furnaces during the winter (although some organizations have successfully merged while maintaining separate sites). The new group may even share equipment and supplies, trading in three broken-down typewriters for one IBM Selectric that really works. Most important, there's greater access to a variety of funding sources. A steady recipient of government contracts might make the perfect partner for an organization known and loved around the foundation conference table.

What to Consider in a Discussion of Mergers

First of all, don't rush. Mergers are often forged in the heat of crisis, and that's why they can produce some extremely dubious couplings. "If you ask two people why they got married," said the former executive director of one recently merged group, "you'll get very different answers from each partner. A merger is the same. People have different needs, and different reasons for their actions."

Each party should define its goals for the merger in terms

of its own self-interest, enlightened by the organizational mission. This will certainly mean consulting a lawyer and forming new bylaws as well as a joint governing Board. Mergers represent program planning on a gigantic and intense scale. They should be neither rejected out of hand, nor precipitously embraced, but rather weighed and studied as a move that will invariably transform the face, and possibly the character, of organizational life.

Many mergers occur only after years of courtship and discussion, once everyone is comfortable with the style and substance of the prospective partners. If you have the leisure to dally, so much the better. A one-year test period, followed by a review of the merger goals, should be built in if at all possible.

In any case, you should consider the following factors:

Shared Vision

Wise mergers unite aspirations as well as organizations. The Boards of merging groups must explore not only their respective programs, but their hopes and dreams—the essence to be retained regardless of the organizational shake-up. In the best cases, the new whole proves greater than the sum of its parts; it stretches the organizational imagination. When funding in the community arts world bottomed out in San Francisco in the mid-1970s, for example, Talespinners (a theater company serving seniors) joined the child oriented Make-A-Circus to form Feedback Productions. The result was a unique blend of arts and social service that soon touched people of almost every age.

Scrupulous Clarity in the Agreement

Mergers require confidence. "If you ask what one thing made it work," said the executive of one merged agency, "I'd answer that it was the good faith and trust between both of our groups." The other factor in mergers that stick seems to be the precision and forthright attitude that characterize the original agreement. All involved should understand what they're getting themselves into, and what they're up against. The prospective action must be thrashed out in meetings, committed to paper, analyzed in every nuance, and then signed by both parties when a complete understanding is reached.

A Fair Alignment of Power

Inevitably, someone will be disenfranchised. In many cases, Board members of a merging organization prove happy to climb out from under the burden. At other times, debate will rage over the distribution of power. Ultimately, it all boils down to Board representation. When East Oakland's San Antonio Neighborhood Health Center merged with La Clinica de la Raza, both organizations accepted the need for compromise. At the time, many small clinics were discussing mergers in terms of equal Board representation, regardless of the group's sizes. But since La Clinica was nearly five times larger than the San Antonio center, the two agencies settled upon a reasonable compromise affording the San Antonio center one-third of the open slots on the new Board, thus blending the vision of the two organizations while maintaining an adequate balance of power.

FACING THE NOT-SO-BITTER END

Drastic change *can* save an organization. Reorganizations and mergers are survival tools—welcome, though usually unexpected, last-ditch efforts. However, they have limitations. After all the struggles, schemes, renewed commitment, and reconstructed hopes, there will be times when you can't go on. There will be times when you shouldn't go on. Discretion will prove the better part of valor. You should know when to quit.

In fact, the nonprofit sector as a whole would be better served if more organizations faced the unpleasant truth that their continued existence may not really matter. The case for "organized abandonment," as Thomas Wolf phrases this ultimate retrenchment, is not considered seriously enough by many organizations. There are a number of very good reasons why struggling, once-powerful, and even successful nonprofit groups should consider giving up the ghost.

• You've fulfilled your mandate. The war is over. And you've won. It's time to congratulate yourselves, pack up, and move on to the next struggle. (But of course, like the March of Dimes, which took on birth defects once polio was virtually eliminated from the United States, you could always lend your unusually effective organization to the pursuit of another, related goal. . . .)

• You've outlived your usefulness. Nobody cares if you disappear. Over the years, the once-mighty rush of clients has dwindled into a tiny stream of old friends and nostalgic patrons. Even your staff and Board are bored by your activities. The organization has grown insular, ignored by the public it claims to serve, and resistant to change.

• You're broke. There are only two major funders in town and they're broke too. The executive spends most of his day fending off creditors. The IRS drops by with questions about some unpaid payroll taxes. You've donated generously, hit up all your friends, and fundraised endlessly, but you still can't balance the books.

• Your organization has disintegrated beyond hope. You've lost three executive directors during the past year and would fire the fourth, but nobody else wants the job. Board membership has declined 75 percent, and nobody has the will to push the organization back into useful shape. You haven't seen a client in weeks, and your assets are so meager that no other organization would dream of a merger.

How to Dissolve

As we've stressed repeatedly, the assessment of your organization's usefulness is the basis of all planning and evaluation. All of us working in organizations, no matter how healthy, should regularly ask ourselves: If we went under today, what difference would it make? Let's assume that you have asked the question. Repeatedly. And the answer is decidedly negative.

How do you begin to dissolve? First of all, who decides?

The power to dismantle an organization rests with the Board of Directors. Remember, whether or not you've actually incorporated, you can't just walk away. There are legal, financial, and moral implications tied to the dissolution. (Even in the most moribund organization, there's bound to be some flicker of pulse. And as responsible Board members, you've got to decide when to turn off the respirator.) But while the Board must take responsibility for burying the dream, there are a number of other parties that must be considered.

Staff, Members, and Volunteers

These people should be the first to know. Don't let them read about it in the papers, and don't assume they know already. Even if they do, they deserve a face-to-face explanation and a chance to ask questions. And of course, your staff needs to be given sufficient time to look for new jobs, or even to decide if they want to try reconstituting the goals of the old group within a new organizational framework. You'll need to depend on these people to walk the last mile with the organization, tying up loose ends and fulfilling final responsibilities. There will be stress involved and considerable emotion. This is not a time to let the internal communications systems break down.

The State

The laws governing the dissolution of nonprofit agencies vary among states. The Board should assign a committee to investigate the requirements of your state and, if necessary, to seek legal assistance in unraveling what may prove to be complicated codes. In most cases, you will need to contact the state attorney general as well as any offices handling taxes or employee benefit records. You'll also need to submit formal articles of dissolution. If you've filed for bankruptcy or have otherwise attracted attention from the legal system, you'll find that your dissolution proceedings will grow appreciably more complex. (Almost certainly, you'll need a lawyer.) In any case, approach these chores with care and precision. Incongruous as it may seem, the construction of one last plan and timetable is necessary. You'll need to take into account all final tasks, assigning them to Board and staff, and follow them through to the end. While omissions and errors may seem inevitable in your rush to disband, they may very well return to haunt you long after the organization has been forgotten and you've moved on to other projects.

The Federal Government

Oddly enough, the federal government (which certainly made you turn backward somersaults for your block grant) doesn't ask a great deal more from you once you've complied with state regulations. However, you must notify the IRS that you have disbanded your corporation by submitting a final return, using the annual Form 990. The taxman's chief concern is that you have distributed your organization's tax-exempt assets for continued charitable use. (In their eyes, the worst scenario would have you dividing the assets among Board members, as a reward for their labors over the years.) Again, you are advised to check with your local IRS office regarding any additional regulations.

Creditors

No doubt, you'll end up owing money. If your financial management system was a contributing factor in the collapse of the organization, then you may even have some trouble determining *whom* and *how much* you owe. In addition to final checks issued to all employees, this matter of settling past debts should be given top priority. You will also be required to publish an announcement in your local newspaper stating that you are going out of business and all debts and claims should be immediately filed with your office. Perhaps more complicated may be the resolution of grants and service contracts which are left uncompleted. These should be negotiated on a case-by-case basis.

The Community

Finally, and of greatest importance, you must notify the community in which you operate that you intend to disband. In fact, this probably should be one of your first actions once the Board has set firmly upon dissolution. In a sense, public notification will serve as one final check on your judgment as a Board. Who knows? Perhaps you'll encounter an underground wave of opposition that will rise up into new support for your organization's activities. Perhaps you'll be gratified to find out that the community won't *let* your organization go gentle into that good night. Maybe an appropriate candidate for a merger will appear.

Your organization deserves an honorable end. The people who depend upon your services should be notified soon enough so that they can make new arrangements. And in all cases, you should strive for a forthright attitude that allows your organization to die with the dignity and trust that it enjoyed during its lifetime.

A Final Note About Endings

"It felt lousy, but it felt great!" summed up the publisher of a now-defunct progressive educational journal. "We told all our writers in November that January would be the last issue. We paid everyone, fulfilled all our contracted ad commitments, and said farewell to our readers in our final issue editorial. We worked out a deal with another educational magazine so that our subscribers would receive one free copy and the opportunity to renew at a discount. Our foundation and corporate funders were satisfied that we'd done as well as we could. They've even suggested that they might fund special issues from time to time. Right now, it's good to be out from under that $2,000 monthly negative cash flow that we just couldn't seem to shake."

That seems to say it all. You'll feel depressed. And relieved. And then guilty about feeling relieved. It's only natural. The organization was an important part of your life.

Moreover, the goals which motivated your participation were perhaps an essential part of your personal identity. You knew who you were by the company you kept, and by the strength and consistency of your actions. And now you've surrendered to expediency, practicality, and a cold, cold bottom line.

Or have you? The end of an era should not be confused with an end to personal commitment and the values and vision that led you to form, join, or contribute to the organization. It may not help at this moment to remember that nothing lives forever; but it's true. To everything there is a season. More important now is to find a new, vital, promising vehicle to carry your rededicated effort.

ADDITIONAL SOURCES

Humanscale by Kirkpatrick Sale. 1980. Perigee Books, New York, NY.

Stimulating, eclectic discourse on the problems of bigness. Running to an improbable 523 pages, Sale makes the case for reasonable limitations to serve human-sized needs.

Merger: A Guide to the Merger Process for Voluntary Human Service Agencies by David Grossman. 1981. Greater New York Fund/United Way, 99 Park Avenue, New York, NY.

An excellent compact guide to the problems of mergers, complete with a number of case studies examining various kinds of nonprofit mergers.

"Thinking the Unthinkable: Should We Go On?" by Tom Boyd. *The Grantsmanship Center News*, Nov./Dec. 1982. The Grantsmanship Center, 1031 South Grand Avenue, Los Angeles, CA 90015.

One of the few works in contemporary nonprofit literature that grapples with the question that we all want to ignore.

* *

THE FUTURE OF NONPROFIT ORGANIZATIONS

Five immodest proposals

"**Where do we start?**"
"**Everywhere at once!**" —*Tout Va Bien*, Jean-Luc Godard

Throughout the course of this book, we've tried to suggest methods for alleviating the most common problems in nonprofit life. We've stressed the importance of building your organization around a clear purpose and achievable goals. We've pointed to the relentless need for dependable financial resources. And we've urged staff, managers, and Boards to cultivate basic skills, while expanding their sense of the possible.

But sound management in the nonprofit sector requires something more than the aggregate mastery of critical skills. At the heart of our sector lies an essential contradiction. And that contradiction must be understood and accommodated—if not actually resolved—if we are to achieve the effectiveness that we so strongly desire. For it seems that in the nonprofit world, we're often simultaneously engaged in opposing quests.

On one hand, we want to soothe the sting of society's harshest realities. We aim to buffer discontent and reform corrupt and ineffectual institutions. We're the salve—or, as our critics might charge, the inadequate Band-Aid—used to treat our nation's severest social ills.

On the other hand, we yearn to tear down these same institutions, and then rebuild them by a different design. We seek not to ameliorate suffering, but to eliminate it. We aim not to quell discontent, but to harness its energy. In the end, some of us owe less to the reformer than the revolutionary.

Add another title to the list of epithets characterizing our nonprofit world: the Schizophrenic Sector.

Many of the questions that cleave communities most mercilessly are those raised and articulated by nonprofits: growth or no growth, a nuclear power plant or not, how should schools and neighborhoods be integrated, where will the halfway house be located? Beyond these specific conflicts lurk the larger issues that define our sector. They represent the forest which we must constantly regard as we individually go about tending our organizational trees. And in the dark of this forest, we must take care not to bump headfirst into the contradictions. As often as not, we will opt for the necessary, if sometimes uncomfortable, accommodations and compromises.

The following proposals are made in response to the complicated demands of our sector. Like all of our efforts, their success will require hard work, dazzling coordination, bulldog tenacity, and the instincts of a riverboat gambler. Given the importance of our goals, both institutional and personal, we have no other choice than to try to grapple with these forces that now affect us all.

1. LEARN HOW THE NONPROFIT SECTOR WORKS

"Today the independent sector stands about where the commercial sector stood in the centuries before we knew why it worked," writes Richard Cornuelle. "Its performance is uneven because it works by accident." While we may dispute the degree to which the marketplace appears comprehensible, it is still clear that the path to understanding the nonprofit world has long been obscured by myth, neglect, and inappropriate comparisons to the other two sectors. Even among experienced nonprofit administrators, confusion often presides over their organization's purpose, constituency, and even language. Over and over we hear the same words: community, service, cultural identity, constituency. What do they really mean?

Take the word "community." It's been with us since the 14th century, and flies like a banner from the ramparts of most small nonprofit groups, but seldom do we really understand the implications of its usage. "What is most important," writes the British critic Raymond Williams, "is that unlike all other terms of social organization (state, nation, society, etc.) it seems never to be used unfavorably and never to be given any positive opposing or distinguishing term. . . . It was when I suddenly realized that no one ever used 'community' in a hostile sense that I saw how dangerous it was." The point is that we must begin to examine even the most basic premises upon which our sector is founded. From there, we may eventually construct some useful theories about nonprofit life that will keep our actions right on target.

• The universities can come to our aid. For the most part, the academic disciplines of economics, political science, and sociology have either minimized or altogether missed the historical importance of the nonprofit sector. However, there are promising signs of change. Recently business schools within the large universities have begun to offer nonprofit concentrations within their graduate programs. Today at Yale University, we find the most encouraging development of all: the founding of the Program on Nonprofit Organizations (PONPO), which has been attracting visiting scholars since 1979 and producing working papers available to the public on everything from nonprofit law, evaluation, and organizational behavior to "the de facto nonprofit sector in Yugoslavia."

• Perhaps most important, we must talk among ourselves. We need to learn about one another's motivations, tactics, and analyses of local problems until we are capable of translating the success of a neighbor's organization into a language that our own community can understand. When appropriate, we can form local support groups to share knowledge and expertise. Consider the example of nonprofit executives in a large metropolitan center who spontaneously organized a series of monthly lunches to discuss their professional problems. Or the flourishing membership coalitions of dance, theater, and visual artists, which provide joint promotion, audience development, advocacy, and other services.

• Larger organizations, with more history and experience, must be approached and encouraged to consult with smaller, newer groups. Already many United Way chapters across the country have expanded their traditional role as funding sources to become constituency service organizations. They now offer a variety of new services to recipients, such as planning, budgeting, and promotion. And coalitions of nonrecipients are approaching the United Way to explore ways in which these services might be spread more broadly throughout the nonprofit community.

• We can make our own contributions to the excellent practical and theoretical work published in trade magazines like *The Grantsmanship Center News, Community Jobs,* and *The Organizer*. We can extend the influence of sophisticated technical assistance organizations operating throughout the nation such as The Support Center and The Youth Project. Our sector drones on endlessly about "networking" and "building partnerships," oftentimes because we imagine that this is what funders want to hear. Now we must approach one another with greater honesty and clear intent. We must become our own best teachers.

2. PROMOTE COOPERATION BETWEEN GOVERNMENT, BUSINESS, AND THE VOLUNTARY SECTOR

"Few truisms are so firmly implanted in the American consciousness as the notion that our economy is a private-enterprise one," states economist Eli Ginzberg. "The fact is that it is not. It is private and public, profit-making and not-for-profit: a pluralistic economy of private enterprise, nonprofit institutions and government." Even among those who understand the nature of our strangely hybrid society, we find only a distant perception of how the three sectors might work in harmony, complementing one another's strengths while taking the sour edge off their well-known, respective weaknesses. Today we often find government, business, and nonprofit organizations locked in conflict, duplicating services, competing unproductively for a limited or cash-poor market, and generally leaving behind a trail of waste and frustration. Clearly, the three sectors need to coordinate their efforts. Improvements will be slow, even evolutionary. We don't yet understand how to create an effective balance among the three sectors, because we have only quite recently begun to think about them as independent forces. However, there are a few obvious places to begin.

• The federal government might join the effort. For example, while the U.S. Department of Health and Human Services has declared that self-help groups will need to double in number by 1990 to make up for federal cuts in mental health programs alone, there has been little thought about what form, size, purpose, or even funding might direct this growth. In general, the government ignores the nonprofit sector, only to drop a load of responsibilities into its lap whenever convenient. The little attention we do receive usually comes in the form of critical reaction, prompted by congressional reservations about our immunity to certain taxes, our social agenda, or the role of private foundations in forming public policy. At the very least, we need a national survey investigating the dimensions, condition, and future of the nonprofit world. From there, we might begin to construct the logical routes to reach policy analysts, lawmakers, and the Oval Office.

• Government can also benefit by turning to the nonprofit sector to supply services historically managed by the public sector. In fact, today we find dozens of cities contracting for recreation, day-care, and health services from independent nonprofit groups. In Portland, Oregon, both the county nursing home and mental health clinics have been transferred to community groups. In Berkeley, California, nonprofit organizations handle the weekly schedule of glass and newspaper recycling. This principle can also be expanded from the local level into state and federal government. As a general proposition that might sit well with both conservatives and progressives, the federal government could propose to halt the expansion of selected government services in favor of spending equal amounts through independent community contractors. By resisting the temptation to bloat government bureaucracy, yet attending to the needs of citizens, lawmakers and administrators might still hit upon a method of grass roots community control that is both equitable and effective.

• Funding could also improve from the coordinated efforts of businesses. When President Reagan claimed that private enterprise could compensate for substantial cuts in federal spending, he must have been thinking about the tax laws which allow corporations to write off up to 10 percent of their adjusted gross profits. But of course, nobody takes advantage of the law. An extremely generous company might give away up to 2 percent. The oil companies, whose declarations of beneficence we witness nightly on public television, give considerably less than 1 percent. In saying that there is room for improvement, we master understatement. In some locales, led by the strong example of Minneapolis, responsible business leaders have formed "5 Percent Clubs" to encourage corporate funding of nonprofit groups. Our task as nonprofit supporters is to find businesspeople in our own communities with the vision and courage to make similar proposals, and the energy and commitment to carry them out. With corporations, peer pressure is the best lever on the reluctant or underdeveloped conscience.

• The next federal jobs bill should include provisions for nonprofit employers. While it is true that the 1970s CETA program employed thousands of workers in the nonprofit sector, they all entered, so to speak, through the back door. The CETA program was intended to stimulate jobs for the "hardcore unemployed" in business and industry. When the for-profit world showed small interest in Congress' designs, the CETA regulations were gerry-rigged to favor the most willing taker: the small, nonprofit, community organization. Of course, the needs and capabilities of most community organizations hardly matched those of the Ford Motor Company. And as a result, many of the employment programs failed miserably at their first intent: permanent employment. The ignominious demise of CETA put numerous nonprofit workers in the unemployment lines, and left their shortsighted organizations shorthanded. The next time around, we should lobby for a jobs bill that will truly suit our needs as small, independent, nonprofit organizations. In fact, the goal of full employment may only be possible if we finally come to recognize the variety and depth of job development resources that are to be found in the independent sector.

3. FIND NEW WAYS TO ENCOURAGE AND REWARD VOLUNTEERS

Individuals, as we've stressed throughout this book, constitute the heart of the voluntary sector. Private donations of time and money fire the nonprofit world with its crusading zeal, its sense of urgency, its tenacity. "Neighborhoods can't win defensive battles," argue David Morris and Karl Hess in their book, *Neighborhood Power*. The same can be said for the entire voluntary sector. Only through the continuing effort of that most famous and sought-after supporter, the average citizen, can we keep our sector on the offensive—providing services, asking questions, and making trouble when necessary. To this end, we need:

• Changes in the current tax laws that will encourage low- and middle-income people to make financial contributions to voluntary organizations. At present, the laws favor the upper classes already accustomed to writing off substantial portions of their annual expenditures. However, if the nonprofit sector is to remain healthy and realize its potential as an instrument of democratic endeavor, it must be accountable to every level of our society. The only way to extend accountability is to give poor and middle-income people the same financial incentives to contribute as those enjoyed by their more affluent counterparts. Waldemar Nielsen has struck upon the immensely sensible idea of allowing every citizen to take a standard deduction from his or her Federal income tax, say $50 for an individual, $100 for a joint return, for contributions made to tax-exempt organizations. This could add billions of dollars to the nonprofit sector each year, while circumventing the costly bureaucratic tangle of foundation and government appropriations.

• And finally, in order to make any of these changes possible, we need an improved attitude toward giving—a promotional face-lift for the entire concept. We need to foster a new, progressive spirit of tithing, or donating a fixed percentage of our personal annual income to the organizations and causes that we truly value. (We can learn from the example of several Western religions, whose members tithe in order to turn special interests and social concerns into effective action, lasting institutions, and political power.) Giving should become commonplace throughout all levels of society, the rule rather than the exception. And it must be emphasized that our generosity as individuals is not meant to relieve government of its obligations. Rather, the well-planned gift should serve as an essential requirement for membership in a just and caring society.

4. TAKE INITIATIVE TO HELP FUNDERS BE MORE EFFECTIVE

We spend too much of our time searching for funding. Not that we have much choice in the matter. As things stand, we either produce the cash necessary to run our programs or we go out of business. Fundraising is a constant in our universe. But a few simple changes could make this fact so much easier to bear.

• Government funders must realize that most voluntary organizations operate with a very modest cash cushion. They cannot afford to carry sizeable reimbursement costs over a long period of time. The federal government, in particular, is notorious for the molasses-like flow of its grant payments. Slow reimbursements create disastrous cash flow shortages for small organizations. Both state and federal agencies should commit to a substantial up-front payment on all grants. If they can't trust their subcontractors with, say, 25 percent of the total award, then they shouldn't approve the grant in the first place.

• Foundations should abandon the tired refrain about providing "seed money for innovative projects." First, not every project should be "innovative." Nothing is wrong with a tried and tested program that efficiently accomplishes what it sets out to do. Furthermore, most organizations that are doing a good job today don't need seed money; they need long-term support. Foundations have for years flinched from this uncomfortable truth as though it somehow reflected poorly upon their judgment as funders. Far worse to consider are the thousands of projects that have ended up as footnotes in nonprofit history, thanks to the built-in obsolesence of their fiscal supports.

• Local funding communities, including foundations and corporations, should establish low-and no-interest loan accounts for nonprofit organizations. In an emergency, the non-profit manager finds that he can only rarely secure commercial loans with the uncertain promise of future grants and income; and he can almost never afford the high interest charged by banks. A substantial loan fund can assist groups over the short-term crisis by providing cash to good-risk organizations. Following the emergency, the fund can help administrators reorganize their financial management to avoid future problems. The Corporations/Foundations Arts Loan and Emergency Funds of San Francisco have successfully used this method for more than a half-dozen years. Other communities could learn from their experience.

5. RECOGNIZE OUR COLLECTIVE POWER TO TRANSFORM AMERICAN SOCIETY

Our nonprofit sector draws much of its inspiration, tactics, and meaning from the American populist tradition. At its best, the voluntary sector coalesces around the diverse and unorganized interests of ordinary people. It offers an antidote to hopelessness and oppression—as it did with the settlement house movement in the early part of this century. It provides an organizational structure for alternatives to economic exploitation—as it did for the early farm and consumer cooperatives of the 1800s. From the very beginning of our nation, the opportunity for voluntary association has provided a means of tilting the social and economic scales toward a more humane and equitable balance and has given our people strength, resilience, and the courage to continue.

Today we witness a resurgence of association coupled to a greater understanding of its implications. "Community-based projects in ethnic, minority, poor, and working-class communities represent a new political constituency," writes Harry C. Boyte. "It is a constituency radically different in orientation from the population of dependent *clients* fostered by traditional welfare state programs. The growing community movement represents, first of all, an assertion by the poor and moderate-income people of their right to participate in American society *on their own terms,* through their own efforts."

• To this end, we need to ask political questions to inform our choices about objectives and methods. Are our programs truly connected to our long-term goals? Are our efforts aimed at alleviating a specific problem, or are we merely extending the influence of our organization? Today we must whittle our way down to essentials: What kind of world are we aiming to create, and how will our programs aid in its creation? If we lose sight of the "big issues," our reason to exist is seriously called into question.

• We need to make connections. Agencies coping with the problems of child abuse, drug addiction, and economic development may all be facing the same broad monster: poverty. It will help strategy and evaluation to understand what we have in common—or fail to share—with the service providers, advocates, and organizers down the block. Once we understand our relationship to other groups and causes, we should put it to good use by forming coalitions. A network of diverse community organizations can wield tremendous political clout, if only on the strength of the people it should be able to turn out for public hearings, demonstrations, and of course, elections.

• As individuals, we need to think about the widest implications of our work for our families, our communities, and our world. What are we each prepared to do to ensure a society of both bread and roses, an America of associated plenty? What is our program of change for the next five years? The next twenty? How do we translate the noble but inchoate aims of our organization, or, if you will, our movement, into effective action?

Today our sector derives enormous strength from the combined energy of hundreds of thousands of individuals, and our collective, sometimes reckless refusal to recognize limitations. We are powerful in a way that the other sectors can never be. Tied neither to the need to make a profit nor to political fashion and expedience, we possess the might to change the world, bit by bit, program by program, one hand helping another. Finally, the only real question facing us is this: To what extent are we willing to invoke the power that is ours?

APPENDIX A

* *

Nonprofit Technical Assistance Organizations

While much training and self-study can be handled informally, there are numerous resources of varying quality that provide a more structured learning environment. Each resource has its own set of advantages and problems, usually balanced in terms of cost, time, location, and content.

Many of these "technical assistance" organizations got their start in the early seventies, as foundations grew increasingly concerned about the lack of basic managerial skills among the people whom they were funding to run important programs. Others grew out of direct constituency needs, often fostered by a "hands-on" approach to solving community problems. The boom years of technical assistance have now drawn to a close, and with them many of the organizations that were responding to the presence of available funding yet offered relatively little in terms of expertise or experience.

The following list does not represent an exhaustive study of the technical assistance field; nor are the organizations ranked preferentially. Rather, it should be approached as a beginner's guide to some of the best available resources operating on a national level.

THE FUNDRAISING SCHOOL
P.O. Box 3237   San Rafael, CA 94902
Purpose: Sessions ranging from several days to a full week covering all aspects of fundraising.

THE GRANTSMANSHIP CENTER
1031 South Grand Avenue   Los Angeles, CA 90015
Purpose: Week-long training sessions held throughout the country on program planning, proposal writing, and other management skills.

THE MIDWEST ACADEMY
600 West Fullerton   Chicago, IL 60614
Purpose: One of the oldest community organizing centers, offering training for neighborhood activists, political researchers, fundraisers, and administrators of membership and social change organizations.

Other groups offering community organizing training include:

- CENTER FOR THIRD WORLD ORGANIZING
  4228 Telegraph Avenue   Oakland, CA 94609

- INDUSTRIAL AREAS FOUNDATION
  675 West Jericho Turnpike   Huntington, NY 11743

- INSTITUTE FOR SOCIAL JUSTICE
  628 Baronne   New Orleans, LA 70113

- ORGANIZE TRAINING CENTER
  1208 Market Street   San Francisco, CA 94103

THE SUPPORT CENTER
1309 L Street, N.W.   Washington, D.C. 20005
Regional Offices: San Francisco, San Diego, Houston, Newark, Oklahoma City, Providence, Rhode Island.
Purpose: Individual consultation and group training covering management, governance, fundraising, and other problem areas for nonprofits.

THE UNITED WAY
United Way chapters operate throughout the United States. Consult your phone directory for the address of your local office.
Purpose: Your local United Way may already offer advice on management, governance, and fundraising. If they don't, they should be encourged to do so. Only a very small number of nonprofit organizations will receive direct financial aid from this

enormous charity, but there's no reason why all of us can't benefit from its connections and expertise.

THE YOUTH PROJECT
1555 Connecticut Avenue N.W.   Washington, D.C. 20036
Regional Offices: Knoxville, San Francisco, Atlanta, Minneapolis.
Purpose: Provides small grants, management, and strategic advice to grass roots social change organizations.

APPENDIX B

* *

College Degree Programs

The newest resource for staff development is the college and university system. In 1984, Independent Sector identified fifty schools offering courses in nonprofit management, and the number is still rising. To date, most of the programs are specialized concentrations within the traditional university fare, like the nonprofit core curriculum within the University of San Francisco's Master in Public Administration program. A few schools, such as the University of California at Davis, offer less conventional options such as a Master's in Community Development; while several graduate schools of social work now run community organizing programs. The best way to survey the current state of undergraduate and graduate education is to check Barron's, Peterson's, or any of the other national directories on higher education available at the public library. They offer brief summaries of program requirements, costs, and resources for further information.

But not everyone will want or need a Ph.D., M.B.A., J.D., or even B.A. And what about people who know precisely what they want to learn, but can't find it within the traditional university catalog?

There are better than two dozen programs throughout the country that adapt very well to the needs of nonprofit managers and organizers. They range from The Union Graduate School's fully accredited Ph.D. program to the more experimental designs of Antioch University. In these cases, the important thing to consider is whether you're interested in an accredited degree program that will carry some weight in more conventional circles or if you're primarily concerned in pursuing a course of study that *you* deem valuable and practical. Upon occasion, you can even do both.

If you're going to investigate the nontraditional degree, then you can do no better than to obtain a copy of *Bear's Guide to Non-Traditional College Degrees* by Dr. John Bear (Mendocino Book Co., P.O. Box 646, Mendocino, CA 95460). Bear's book is the most extensive and timely guide to alternative degree granting programs, complete with clear-eyed warnings on their hazards as well as their glories. Another useful resource is the article "Take Credit for Your Organizing" by Carter Garber and Marty Collier, published in the April 1982 issue of *Community Jobs*. Although slanted toward social change agencies, this excellent guide fully explores the why and how of formal education for nonprofit workers.

BIBLIOGRAPHIC NOTES

* *

Introduction

Among the most useful books investigating nonprofit organizations and the American voluntary spirit are Waldemar A. Nielsen, *The Endangered Sector* (New York: Columbia University Press, 1979); Harry C. Boyte, *The Backyard Revolution* (Philadelphia: Temple University Press, 1980) and *Community Is Possible* (New York: Harper/Colophon, 1984); Richard Sennett, *The Fall of Public Man* (New York: Vintage Books, 1978); Brian O'Connell, ed., *America's Voluntary Spirit* (New York: The Foundation Center, 1983); Richard Cornuelle, *Healing America* (New York: G. P. Putnam's Sons, 1983) and *Reclaiming the American Dream* (New York: Random House, 1965); Allen J. Matusow, *The Unraveling of America* (New York: Harper & Row, 1984); Walter A. Friedlander, *Introduction to Social Welfare* (Englewood Cliffs, N.J.: Prentice-Hall, 1961); Gerald Handel, *Social Welfare in Western Society* (New York: Random House, 1982); Jane Addams, *Twenty Years at Hull House* (New York: The Macmillan Company, 1910); Allen F. Davis, *American Heroine: The Life and Legend of Jane Addams* (Oxford: Oxford University Press, 1973); and of course, Alexis de Tocqueville, *Democracy in America* (New York: Mentor Books, 1956).

A number of magazine articles and organizational publications also proved useful, including: Daniel Ben-Horin and Fenton Johnson, "In the Public Interest" in *California Living*, the *San Francisco Sunday Examiner and Chronicle*, February 19,

1984; Frank Riessman, "Self-Helpers" in *The Nation*, June 2, 1984; "The 1983 Gallup Survey on Volunteering" in *Voluntary Action Leadership*, Winter 1984; Lester M. Salamon, James C. Musselwhite, Jr., and Alan J. Abramson, "Voluntary Organizations and the Crisis of the Welfare State" (Washington, D.C.: The Urban Institute, 1983); The Nonprofit Sector Project, "Progress Reports" (Washington, D.C.: The Urban Institute, Reports #2 and #3, 1982).

1. Another Kind of Boardroom

Several books proved valuable in examining the nonprofit Board and the problems of management. They include: Cyril O. Howe, *The Effective Board* (New York: The Association Press, 1960); Barbara H. Schilling, *Glossary of Tools and Concepts for Nonprofit Managers* (San Francisco: The Management Center, 1981); H. George Frederickson, *New Public Administration* (Alabama: University of Alabama Press, 1980); Thomas Wolf, *The Nonprofit Organization* (Englewood Cliffs, N.J.: Prentice-Hall, 1984); Diane Borst and Patrick J. Montana, eds., *Managing Nonprofit Organizations* (New York: Amacom, 1977); Gerald Zaltman, ed., *Management Principles for Nonprofit Agencies and Organizations* (New York: Amacom, 1979).

The following in-house publications and magazine articles also provided insight into common Board maladies: "Governance and Executive Roles in Nonprofit Organizations" (San Francisco: The Support Center, 1983); and Thomas L. Whisler, "Some Do's and Don'ts for Directors" in *The Wall Street Journal*, March 21, 1983.

2. Who's in Charge Here, Anyway?

The critical issues in nonprofit staffing and organizational design are covered by: Brian O'Connell, *Effective Leadership in Voluntary Organizations* (New York: The Association Press, 1976); Joan Flanagan, *The Successful Volunteer Organization* (Chicago: Contemporary Books, 1981); William G. Scott and David K. Hart, *Organizational America* (Boston: Houghton Mifflin, 1979); Joan M. Hummel, *Starting and Running a Nonprofit Organization* (Minneapolis: University of Minnesota Press, 1980); Michael T. Matteson and John M. Ivancevich, eds., *Management Classics*

(Santa Monica, Calif.: Goodyear Publishing Company, 1981); and Robert Townsend, *Further Up the Organization* (New York: Knopf, 1984).

A number of magazine articles also examined the problems of nonprofit leadership and administration: William L. Bryan, Jr., "Administration of Public Interest Groups" in *The NRAG Papers*, Summer 1977, and "Preventing Burnout in the Public Interest Community" in *The Grantsmanship Center News*, March/April 1981; Susan Thomas, "Team Building Within Your Organization" in *The Grantsmanship Center News*, May/June 1983; *Voluntary Action Leadership*, Summer 1984 (the entire issue concerned the management of volunteers); Paul Desruisseaux, "Nonprofit Groups Want Academe to Help Train Their Administrators" in *Philanthropy*, November 14, 1984; Thomas J. C. Raymond and Stephen A. Greyser, "The Business of Managing the Arts" in *Harvard Business Review*, July–August 1978; Carter Garber and Marty Collier, "Take Credit for Your Organizing" in *Community Jobs*, April 1982; Charles Biggs, "Honing the Edge" in *Community Jobs*, November 1980.

3. *How to Avoid Losing $100,000*

Among the books we turned to for assistance with financial management and record-keeping are: Leon Haller, *Financial Management for Nonprofit Organizations* (Englewood Cliffs, N.J.: Prentice-Hall, 1982); Charles A. Nelson and Frederick J. Turk, *Financial Management for the Arts* (New York: American Council for the Arts, 1975); Robert Lefferts, *The Basic Handbook of Grants Management* (New York: Basic Books, 1983); *Bookkeeping Handbook for Low-Income Citizen Groups*, prepared by the National Council of Welfare (Ottawa: NCW, 1973); and The Support Center, *Budget and Budget Monitoring* and *Fiscal Management* (San Francisco: The URSA Institute, 1983).

4. *Long-range Planning*

In this chapter we relied heavily upon interviews with expert planners in the field as well as several helpful books, including Peter F. Drucker, *The Changing World of the Executive* (New York: Times Books, 1982); and George A. Steiner, "Strategic Managerial Planning," published in 1977 by The Planning/Executive's Institute in Oxford, Ohio.

Several articles were also informative: Kenneth R. Andrews, "Directors' Responsibility for Corporate Strategy" in *Harvard Business Review*, November–December 1980; Peter R. Linkow, "Implementing the Long-Range Plan" in *The Grantsmanship Center News*, January–February 1983; William Weber and Suzanne Weber, "Long-Range Process Planning: The First Cut" in *The Grantsmanship Center News*, July–August 1982.

5. *Fundraising as a Way of Life*

Among the many books available regarding fundraising and the culture of philanthropy, we turned to: Thomas W. Tenbrunsel, *The Fund Raising Resource Manual* (Englewood Cliffs, N.J.: Prentice-Hall, 1982); Waldemar A. Nielsen, *The Big Foundations* (New York: Columbia University Press, 1972); Arthur M. Schlesinger, Jr., *The Coming of the New Deal* (Boston: Houghton Mifflin, 1959); Cicero, *On Moral Obligation (De Officiis)*, translated by John Higginbotham (London: Faber, 1967); David Edward Owen, *English Philanthropy, 1660–1960* (Cambridge: Harvard University Press, Belknap Press, 1964); Richard M. Titmuss, *The Gift Relationship* (New York: Vantage Books, 1971); Kurt Vonnegut, Jr., *God Bless You, Mr. Rosewater* (New York: Dell Publishing Company, 1965); Lewis Thomas, "Altruism" in *Late Night Thoughts on Listening to Mahler's Ninth Symphony* (New York: Viking Press, 1983); and Garrison Keillor, "Jack Schmidt, Arts Administrator" and "Jack Schmidt on the Burning Sands" in *Happy to Be Here* (New York: Penguin Books, 1983).

Also useful are: Tim Sweeney and Michael Seltzer, "Survival Planning for the '80s," a three-part reprint published by *Community Jobs* in Washington, D.C.; and Tom Boyd, "The Business of Business Is . . . Philanthropy" in *The Grantsmanship Center News*, May–June, 1982. And of course, the serious fundraiser can do no better than to regularly read both *The Grantsmanship Center News* (Los Angeles), and *Foundation News* (Washington, D.C.).

6. *From Exxon to Your Next-door Neighbor*

For the methods of fundraising, we turned to George A. Brakeley, Jr., *Tested Ways to Successful Fund Raising* (New York: Amacom); Katy Butler, Laura Bouyea, and Barbara Garza, *Robin Hood Was Right* (San Francisco: The Vanguard Public Foundation, 1977); Joan Flanagan, *The Grass Roots Fundraising Book* (Washington, D.C.: The Youth Project).

A great number of reprints from *The Grantsmanship Center News* (published by The Grantsmanship Center, Los Angeles) proved extremely useful. They include: Joanna Raebel, "Volunteers from Business"; Ron Ridenour, "Federal Funding: The First 200 Years"; Patricia Malo, "The Big Search"; Jack Shakeley, "Community Foundations" and "Exploring the Exclusive World of Corporate Giving." We also profited from "American Business and the Arts," a special section running in *The Christian Science Monitor*, November 7, 1983; and *Grassroots Fundraising Journal* published in San Francisco since 1982.

7. How to Get a Grant

For perspective on proposal writing and foundations we turned to Carol M. Kurzig, *Foundation Fundamentals* (New York: The Foundation Center, 1980).

And once again, several reprints from *The Grantsmanship Center News* were helpful: Norton J. Kiritz, "Program Planning and Proposal Writing, Expanded Version" and "Proposal Checklist and Evaluation Form"; and by the Staff, "How Foundations Review Proposals & Make Grants."

8. Survival Tactics

Information on marketing and self-sufficiency planning can be found in the following books: Patrick J. Montana, *Marketing in Nonprofit Organizations* (New York: Amacom, 1979); Charles Cagnon, *Business Ventures of Citizen Groups* (Helena, Mont.: The Northern Rockies Action Group, 1982); William A. Duncan, *Looking at Income-Generating Businesses for Small Nonprofit Organizations* (Washington, D.C.: Center for Community Change, 1982).

The following articles also provided important perspective: Edward Skloot, "Should Not-for-Profits Go into Business?" in *Harvard Business Review*, January–February 1983; Bradford N. Dewan, "Operation of a Business by Non-Profit, Tax-Exempt Organizations" in *Economic Development and Law Center Report*, published in March/April 1980, by The National Economic Development and Law Center in Berkeley, California; Alan R. Andreasen, "Nonprofits: Check Your Attention to Customers" in *The Grantsmanship Center News* November–December 1982; and Roger Williams, "Why Don't We Start a Profit-Making Subsidiary?" in *The Grantsmanship Center News*, January–February, 1982.

9. When Nobody Knows Your Name

A number of books helped clarify the role of publicity and public relations: Lucile A. Maddalena, *A Communications Manual for Nonprofit Organizations* (New York: Amacom, 1981); Scott M. Cutlip and Allen H. Center, *Effective Public Relations* (Englewood Cliffs, N.J.: Prentice-Hall, 1971); Thomas Wolfe, *Presenting Performances* (New York: American Council for the Arts, 1981); David R. Yale, *The Publicity Handbook* (New York: Bantam Books, 1982).

Also see: "A Handbook on Free Access to Media for Public Service Advertising," published by the Public Media Center in San Francisco.

10. Finessing City Hall

Books dealing with political power and lobbying by nonprofit groups include: Kare Anderson, *Cutting Deals with Unlikely Allies* (Oakland, Calif.: Anderson Negotiations/Communications Press, 1981); George Alderson and Everett Sentman, *How You Can Influence Congress* (New York: E. P. Dutton, 1979); Meg Campbell, Lina Newhouser, and Wade Rathke, eds., *Community Organizing Handbook #2* (Little Rock, Ark.: The Institute for Social Justice, 1977); Standford F. Brandt, *A Layman's Guide to Lobbying Without Losing Your Tax-Exempt Status* (Arlington: Mental Health Association); Saul D. Alinsky, *Rules for Radicals* (New York: Vintage, 1972) and *Reveille for Radicals* (New York: Vintage, 1969); Mark Green, *Winning Back America* (New York: Bantam, 1982); and Si Kahn, *Organizing* (New York: McGraw-Hill, 1982).

We also used the following articles: Tim Sampson, "Coalitions and Other Relations" in *The Organizer*, Fall 1983, published by The Institute for Social Justice, New Orleans; and Richard J. Margolis, "The New Mexican Umbrella" in *Foundation News*, May–June 1984.

11. Expansion and Extinction

The following books dealt with problems of growth, mergers, and closure: Kirkpatrick Sale, *Humanscale* (New York: Perigee Books, 1980); and David Grossman, *Merger* (New York: Greater New York Fund/United Way, 1981).

Also useful was Tom Boyd, "Thinking the Unthinkable" in *The Grantsmanship Center News*, November–December 1982.

Epilogue

Among the valuable books exploring the future of nonprofit organizations are: Robert N. Bellah, Richard Madsen, William M. Sullivan, Ann Swidler, and Steven M. Tipton, *Habits of the Heart* (Berkeley: University of California Press, 1985); David Morris and Karl Hess, *Neighborhood Power* (Boston: Beacon Press, 1975); Alan Gartner, Colin Greer, and Frank Riessman, eds., *Beyond Reagan* (New York: Harper & Row, 1984); Raymond Williams, *Keywords* (Oxford: Oxford University Press, 1976); Karen Feiden and Geoffrey Link, eds., *Surviving the '80s* (San Francisco: Intersection, 1980); and John L. Palmer and Isabel V. Sawhill, eds., *The Reagan Record* (Washington, D.C.: The Urban Institute, 1984).

In addition, we found interesting material in the following magazine articles: Eli Ginzberg, "The Pluralistic Economy of the U.S." in *Scientific American*, December 1976; *Journal of Community Action*, vol. 1, no. 4, 1982 (the entire issue covered community partnerships with business and government); Lester Salamon, "The Future of the Nonprofit Sector" in *The Grantsmanship Center News*, September/December 1984; and *The Progressive*, June 1984, in a special issue on "The New Populism" (in particular, articles by Lawrence Goodwyn, Harry C. Boyte, and Heather Booth and Janet Kelsey).

INDEX

* *